My Day in Heaven
with My Lil' Sister

Quest Delaney

My Day in Heaven with My Lil' Sister

TATE PUBLISHING
AND ENTERPRISES, LLC

Published by Tate Publishing & Enterprises, LLC
127 E. Trade Center Terrace | Mustang, Oklahoma 73064 USA
1.888.361.9473 | www.tatepublishing.com

Tate Publishing is committed to excellence in the publishing industry. The company reflects the philosophy established by the founders, based on Psalm 68:11,
"The Lord gave the word and great was the company of those who published it."

Book design copyright © 2013 by Tate Publishing, LLC. All rights reserved.
Cover design by Allen Jomoc
Cover concept by Quest Delaney
Interior design by Joana Quilantang

Published in the United States of America

ISBN: 978-1-62295-260-1
1. Biography & Autobiography / Personal Memoirs
2. Religion / Christian Life / Death, Grief, Bereavement
13.03.01

Dedication

To my LORD and Savior, Jesus Christ. Without Him I couldn't tell you my experiences. Thank you, God, for letting me come to heaven when I hadn't passed over yet. Sr'love, my dearest angel, I can't wait to see you again, love. I love you so much. I have pure love for you, always!

To my wonderful mother. Your strength lives in me. A mother is a gift given from God. I am so thankful to have such a beautiful mother. I love you, Ma, from the bottom of my heart! Thank you so much for giving birth to me. For forty years of my life you taught me to be strong. You always inspired me. You would say, "Remember where you came from to get to where you are going. Understand there are times you must admit defeat, and start all over, building anew. You must visualize success. To never think or say, "I can't!" Just believe in yourself, and you'll be blessed at obstacles that stand in your way." I have learned and I'm still learning the wonders of life. Thank you from the bottom of my heart for building such an artistic mind of creativity. My spiritual mind has blossomed into such levels. I now understand. What a wonderful combination!

To my dearest father. God placed you in my mother's life. It was love between you and her that created me. Without your creativeness and your artistic abilities, my vision wouldn't have been clear. Thanks for your love, Pops! Much love to you. Thank you both, Mom and Dad.

To my beautiful sister, Ty. You are my world. Without you my spirit wouldn't be the same. We've done everything together since we were three years old. We are one. When I look in the mirror, I not only see me, but you, too! Our love for each other is nothing but heavenly. No one comes closer. You're my beautiful sister and my best friend.

To my little, beautiful sister, "K. Yvonne." You're the first baby I ever fed and held and cared for. I played "Gotta Be Where You Are" by The Jackson 5 so many times. You left us with so many wonderful memories. We will never forget. I keep hearing in my head, "Never Can Say Good-bye" by Michael Jackson over and over again. Thank you for coming back for one more time, and letting me share heaven with you. You always told me I was your idol. I always admired your creativeness, your passion to help others, knowing they couldn't be helped if they didn't help themselves. My world has changed without you in it, but you live in my spirit everyday. I've cried on every page of this book, wishing this was all a bad dream, but it's all real. If I had one more day with you, you could run and jump in my arms again and spin around again and we would just laugh until our stomachs hurt! I miss you so much, and I love you. You'll always be my lil' sis.

To my beautiful children, Devin, Quest, and Kayla: I love you from my heart. I enjoy being your father. You make my soul young and joyful. Sometimes I wish I could go to school with you, play and learn together in class, eat lunch together, have cookie and juice time, and take a nap together. I enjoy being your dad, cracking jokes together. Just to hear your laugh reminds me of "someone special," my little sister. Don't ever say you can't do something. You must believe you can do it. Always!

To my sisters and brothers, Apria, O'Shea, Cierra, and Sabian: I couldn't ask for a much happier family. I love you all with my heart and soul. I'm always there if you need me. Always strive high, no matter what stands in your way. Always believe in yourself. I believe in you!

To my wonderful nephew and niece, J'Waun and Tyshiya: Your mother's passing and going to heaven is something very special. She allowed me to come with her and share that moment with the whole world. Her love lives on through people she touched and our family. There's nothing in the world I wouldn't do for you. You've lost a wonderful mother who gave birth to you. So, please, enjoy life to the fullest. Always thank your mother for bringing you into this world. Your mother tried to help everyone who stood in front of her with a problem. She was some people's angel. Others called her special, but she was an angel, my angel from the first time she took her first breath on earth. I knew she was an angel because of how she came to my father and mother. When you're lonely, just call your mother for guidance. She loved you both so much.

All my love to the Delaneys, Gallmans, Boyds, Apontes, Clarks, Triplines, Hearns, Richardsons, Hollands, Baileys, D. Williams, Fogles, Whitteds, Fielders, Mitchels, Harrisons, Baldizons, Queens, Halls, Mays, McIntosh's, Segals, Michael Jackson, The Jackson's, Thalleys, Manns, D. Crazy, Davis's, Bakers, Hardys, Coles, Newmans, Edwards, Danets, Redlands, Royals, Proctors, Woodards, Bells, Bias, the Wades.

If I forgot anyone, I am so sorry. I still love you, too. All my friends!

Love is the most beautiful feeling you could give to someone special. Tomorrow is not promised. Please love with your heart. I always do. Thank you so much for touching my life and my heart. Enjoy what I wrote because I've cried on every page, some more than others.

To everyone who's ever lost a loved one, this book is dedicated to you.

Acknowledgements

My greatest appreciation and love to my family, but especially to my mother and sister. I'm honored to be loved by you. Without you my heart would be lonely. Your love is so special to me. I thank God every day for you being in my life.

My love for First Baptist Church of Glenarden, Pastor John K. Jenkins, Sr., Rev. Sims, Pastor Duane E. Dickens, Sr., and Minister Billy T. Staton, Jr. and their families. Without your love and belief, this book would have never been possible.

Special love to Kenny Loggins's song "Love Will Follow," which was playing while I wrote this book. Your song means a lot to my heart.

To BeBe and Cee Cee Wynans, your song, "Heaven" speaks to my heart so dearly. My lil' sister and I loved and sang this song together so many times.

To Michael Jackson, whom I love dearly. This book was written before your death. Because of your love and emotion on "Never Can Say Good-bye" and "Got To Be There," I would play them for my lil' sister while she would fall asleep and when she became a young lady. I had no idea that those two songs would mean so much to me.

My love and appreciation to my dear friends. Love from your hearts has made my soul feel so loved and special. My spiritual love, Martina, you were the one who believed in my special gift. Your knowledge and spiritual beliefs has taught me how to express my belief more freely. In 2005, when I shook your hand, you knew that I was special. I was in such denial, but now my spiritual beliefs are free. We never met before, but you told me incredible things about myself. I was blown away from your knowledge. My love for you is pure. I love you so much and your family as well. My admiration and appreciation to Christi. You are one of a kind, let me tell you that first! To Linda Wade, thank you so much for caring about my book. You're an angel at heart, and I love you with every beat of my heart.

To the whole world, tell someone you care about you love 'em. I love the feeling of love.

Much Love World,

Quest Delaney

Table of Contents

Introduction..15

My True Experience...17

Wednesday, February 18, 2009 8:52 a.m. 19

The Phone Call!...21

I'm Dreaming 23

The Ride 27

Is God Telling Me Something?......................................29

The Waiting Room...31

Death..35

Pages of Tears..37

Pages of Tears..41

The Blueprint...43

She's Alive! 45

Spirit to Spirit...47

Is There a Heaven?...49

Her Smile 51

To Keisha 53

Mad At God..55

My Little Sister Talking...59

Paradise 63

Paradise Island...65

Tricks in the Air 67

Angel Clouds..69

Welcome Her Back 71

We Entered Heaven 73

What "Quest" Means...77

Paradise Wings 81

Roses That Love 85

The Kingdom..87

Inside the Palace...91

In Love with an Angel..93

God Spoke to My Lil' Sister...99

Pages ofTears...103

I Believe..105

At the Table 107

Teach Me 109

Mom, Have a Seat...111

Clouds 113

What Do Numbers Mean? 115

The Last Walk...117

Lost without My Lil' Sister 119

 Pages of Tears..121

Ask for an Angel...123

Angel Bariel..125

Our Last Tear Together 127

Angels Communicating...129

When My Lil' Sister Died..135

Questions People Ask Me 139

Trying to Move On 143

Dad...147

Mother 149

My Grandmother 155

Believe 164

Seventeen..165

My First Out-Of-Body Experience...............................169

No Love...171

My Spiritual Dream..177

Preface

To have a little sister is the most wonderful feeling in the world. A special gift from God. I have so much love for her. My heart will never be the same without her, but her love and her love for others whom she touched with her heart will Live Forever.

Introduction

If someone close to you passed away suddenly
Your mother
Father
Grandparents
Brother
Sister
Uncle
Aunt
Wife/Husband
Girlfriend/Boyfriend

*And t*hey came back to you for a day, would you love them even more? Love makes the heart smile, so tell that someone who means the world to you, "I love you so much." Maybe that person is going through problems, had a hard day, or just wants to hear those beautiful words. Always love from deep within. From within, love will bloom.

My True Experience

On February 18, 2009, at 7:12 a.m.

My Lil' sister, K. Yvonne was found face down on the floor in her bedroom, motionless with no pulse! Her kids were going to school that morning, but they overslept and waited for their mother to wake them up like every morning for ten years. They were used to that morning routine.

On February 18, 2009, their world had changed. As they awoke by themselves, and with a slow glance, they noticed their mother motionless facedown on the floor. She didn't have a pulse, and she was blue all over. Paramedics were called to the house where they tried CPR for several minutes. They could not get a pulse from my lil' sister, their mother. A phone call was placed to my other sisters along with my parents who came to the house immediately.

They all watched the paramedics try everything to save my lil' sister, Keisha. The outcome was very devastating for the entire family.

My lil' sister and I were very close. We were so spiritual we felt we could read each other's thoughts. When she was five years old, I would pick her up from daycare. Every time we walked home, we would look up at the sky. Every time we would pass the clouds. They looked so close. It was a perfect picture.

MLS asked, "Where is heaven? Can we fly there or take a bus? How does heaven look? What should I wear? Can we go see heaven one day? Can we go together one day, just us two, big brother? Can we…" After her passing, she asked God if she could bring me with her so that we could see heaven together. God told her, "Yes, you can. Go get your big brother, Quest, so you can share this experience together, so Quest can enlighten others of his journey to and from heaven."

This is my true experience of my day in heaven with my lil' sister.

Wednesday, February 18, 2009 8:52 a.m.

The Phone Call!

Q: "What's up?"

The phone rang, and I could hear my little sister crying in the background. "Can you meet us at P.G. Hospital because Keisha is not breathing." The crying in the background got louder. "Mommy and sis are not doing well, so uh, please meet us at the hospital, okay? Love ya'll!"

I'm Dreaming

When I heard the message, my heart dropped. As I sat on my sofa, totally numb, I called my sister, Ty, just to make sure I wasn't dreaming. Again I was told, as she answered the phone (crying uncontrollably).

" Keisha wasn't breathing, Q! She wasn't breathing! She was lying on the floor when the kids found her motionless. Please get here soon! Please! I love you."

"Okay, I love you more," I replied.

At that moment all I could hear was my heartbeat. I couldn't hear anything else.

I walked to the bathroom and ran the water. As I lowered my hand under the faucet, all I could hear was my heartbeat louder and louder. As I listened to my heartbeat, I noticed my pupils were large. When I looked in the mirror, my pupils didn't adjust to the light at all. I could smell the water from the faucet. I cold hear this buzzing noise from my living room. There was a fly in the blinds of the window. *How can all this be happening to me now? What is going on with me?* I kept asking myself.

I heard chimes in the air, but the ones hanging on my balcony weren't moving at all. I asked myself what was going on. As I stood there amazed and confused, I called my sister again.

She answered the phone, "Where are you?"

I replied, "I'm coming! How long was she not breathing?"

"A very long time! Too long, Quest, too long! She's not going to make it, but we're praying."

The EMT brought Keisha downstairs on the stretcher. Ty explained that there were seven of them. Four were carrying her motionless body. The other three were pumping her chest. In the background, I could hear, "Come on, Keisha," they were saying over and over again. Ma was crying hard. Screams filled the airwaves. I knew that she was gone. Ty also explained that her hands, lips, and feet were blue. "She's gone."

"Keisha!"

"She's gone. Please hurry up and get here, please!"

"I'm leaving right now. I love ya!" I said as I hung up the phone.

I will never forget those two words ever again. I started to cry. I was trying to hold my tears back, but I just couldn't. I told myself to take a deep breath. As I took my deep breath, I heard someone's voice telling me to take another. This voice sounded just like MLS's voice. Impossible! Impossible, I thought to myself! So, I told myself it wasn't her voice.

In a whispered voice I heard, "Hey, Big Brother, it's me. You coming to see me?"

"Keisha!" I shouted out to myself, as if she was standing in my living room! I was walking toward my front door. *Why am I tripping out?* I thought to myself. *No! I'm hallucinating! Yeah, I am!* I looked around again as if Keisha was right in front of me.

"Hey, Big Brother!"

"Who is that?" I shouted out. I turned down the volume to the radio just to make sure I wasn't hallucinating, and before I left my house, I could hear Keisha's voice again. This time really clear, "That's it, Big Brother."

"What do you mean, that's it?" I shouted with tears running down my face. I needed some fresh air because I felt like I was losing my mind. I tried to block what I just heard out of my mind, but walking outside wasn't the same! This time, wow! As I walked outside, all my senses were working on overload. As I walked outside, I could smell snow in the air. It wasn't supposed to snow that day. I made eye contact with this bird flying past me. She was flying in slow motion. I felt like I could hear this bird's thoughts. She was looking for a place to make a bird's nest. I could hear every flap as if this bird was trying to tell me something. She turned her head, and we connected eye to eye. Without thinking about it, I could zoom in closer and see every feather move so smoothly. I noticed the dry grass dangling from her beak. As she looked to build her nest, I could feel a connection with that one glance. That connection I felt was real. So real that same bird flew around the back of my house and made a nest in a fake tree I had on my patio, later producing three little birdies. *How amazing*, I thought.

The Ride

At 9:01 a.m., I got in my truck and "Halo" was playing. I turned off the radio so my mind would be much clearer, but again I heard, "This is it, Big Brother" in a jovial tone.

I drove to the hospital thinking, "This is for her." I'm not a negative person at all. I think positively all the time. My heart knew this was it. My mind, I thought was playing tricks on me. But why? I thought, why me? My mind was thinking why me and my heart and soul were telling me, "I'm sorry she's gone." I started thinking about the first songs I played for her, Michael Jackson's "Never Can Say Good-Bye," and "Got to Be There." Those two songs played in my head until I arrived at the hospital. All I could think about was when my lil' sister was five years old. She was so adorable and had the funniest laugh. Her laugh would make me laugh.

Parking my truck was so hard to do at that moment. Knowing when I got out, what was to come. I could smell snow in the air Again, I could hear my lil' sister's voice.

"It's okay, Big Brother. I'm okay. You're here now to care and protect me. Like always, right? Just like when I was little."

I thought, "Why can I hear this? Why?" Holding back tears, I started walking toward the hospital doors. Holding back my tears, I just wanted a happy outcome for my lil' sis.

"Please God! Please help my lil' sister. She's too young to die. She always helped people. You have to help her, God! You must! Please!"

Is God Telling Me Something?

As I entered the waiting room, I looked around. I didn't even notice my family. I didn't see them at all. But I could hear people crying. I knew who was going to cry and who was very upset. I knew who was praying to God quietly to themselves. To hear all this was amazing to me. I was sill in denial of the gift I had, but I did know my spirit level was reaching a level I have never experienced before. I was scared. I found myself taking deep breaths.

Everyone was talking to me, wanting me to help them, guide them to a place I didn't know. I looked around at everyone in the waiting room, but no one was moving their mouths. How was it that I could I hear all these people's thoughts? "Just believe," I told myself. How was I able to hear and feel their pain. I've always been able to do this, but I just told myself not to. I really didn't understand why now I must go through this. Was God telling me something? As I entered the fourth floor, I heard what I thought were drums. But it wasn't the sound of drums I heard; it was my family's heartbeats. All of them were sitting in the waiting room.

The Waiting Room

As I entered the waiting room, around 9:13 a.m., the room was quiet and very cold. My lil' sister's children, my mother and father, and my other sisters were all sitting in the room nervously waiting.

My brothers were at school and would arrive later. My nephew's grandmother (Ms. Ruth) was also with the family. Everyone in this room I loved deeply. I sat watching my sister Ty wiping my mother's tears. It was so hard to watch as every tear came down her lovely face. It was too much to bear. One glance at my mother made me feel helpless. I'd never seen my mother cry. Never! My whole life flashed before me as I blinked. My mother had tears in her eyes when she gave birth to my lil' sister, "Keisha." Those were tears of joy. Now she has tears of sorrow, knowing that her little girl whom she gave birth to may not be here with her anymore. I looked around the room and again, I could feel everyone's spirit.

Every one of us felt helpless. We knew that this was up to God and the medical team. I couldn't help but think about our last conversation. Keisha had asked me on Tuesday if Goofy was a dog or a walrus. We laughed so hard I could still hear her laugh. "So, God," I prayed, "I'm asking you to help my sister through this nightmare. Please God, she's young and beautiful, and she's a mother, daughter, and aunt. We need her, God! Please! My world won't be the same without her. We used to always talk about going to heaven, but this is too soon, God! Please, not now! Please, not now. Please," I begged.

I was hoping for the doctors to tell us some uplifting information, but as time was ticking by so slowly, I started reminiscing about my lil' sister and with every tear streaming down my face, I tried to show my coolness and calmness, but it faded away, and I drifted away to happiness with my lil' sister.

Keisha was the first baby I had ever held. She was more than my lil' sister. She was my everything: my spiritual lil' baby sister. I felt instant love for her. She was special to our family and to me. I learned how to love, care, and share my feelings with others because of my love for her. I loved to look at her all the time. I could see myself in her which I thought was amazing. She had the most beautiful eyes. I would give her my heart if I had to. We connected spiritually. Spiritual love is a different type of love. I loved her as my lil' sister too, but there was something different about my lil' sister that I felt in my heart. I want to say I felt what she felt deep within, and being that she was my first baby I ever held, that was pure love. She was a gift from God. I've learned how to feed her, bathe her and clothe her. I taught her my good traits of life.

I could feel and hear everyone's heartbeats speed up. Everyone's eyes looked so enlarged. My dad knew I could hear him say to himself, "Nah, not my Keisha-Weisha"

He was trying to stay calm for us. His coolness was taken over by deep emotions and thoughts that he and Keisha only knew about. Ty was very sad and taking this very hard. My parents and she were there in the apartment while Keisha lay lifeless.

The door opened! The room became very cold. The doctor entered with his assistant. I could tell this wasn't going to be good. The doctor's demeanor told it all. As a police officer, I knew. The doctor stood there, and I could tell it was hard for him. His throat was very dry when he spoke. There was no eye contact at first.

As he looked around the room at all of us, he rested his eyes on my parents. He said, "When she came in, she wasn't responding to CPR. We tried another test. I thought that he was going to say that the test was successful, but he said, "I'm sorry. We tried everything. She never had a pulse." The crying soon became louder and louder as the news sank in.

I tried hard not to cry, holding back my tears. The doctor said, "Two at a time can go in to see her." My parents went first, comforting each other. I held Ty, as she cried on my chest. Every tear seemed to go through my chest, touching my heart. My heartbeat seemed to comfort Ty. As tears flooded my eyes, I couldn't help but to remember my lil' sister just being here laughing with me, Dad talking to my mom, and remembering my last conversation with Keisha asking me about Goofy!

To hear she never had a pulse meant she was never coming back, and all I could do was think of her from two to five years old—many of her happiest moments.

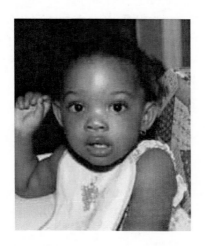

Death

My mind went blank, and my soul drifted away. We sat and comforted each other, but there were no words spoken. We looked at each other with tears streaming down our faces.

I could not fathom the loss of my lil' sister or my other sisters for that matter. I had thought about dying of old age, not when at twenty-nine and healthy. To think Keisha and I would never hug each other again. Who was going to laugh at all my jokes? Every day she told me she loved me. It was a special way that she would say it, and smile afterwards. I would say, "I love you, Keisha," and she would say, "Mmmmm, I love you too, Big Brother."

The look on my parents's face was unforgettable. My dad has hazel eyes. When he came back in the waiting room, his eyes were lime green. Both parents' pupils were dilated, the same as my own when I was home. To see both parents crying was unbearable. It was so painful for me to look at them. My mother's face has a very beautiful tone, but this day her face was pale, her pupils enlarged, hands shaking uncontrollably. I hugged my mother. I felt like her baby again.

Pages of Tears

When my lil' sister was three years old, there was a nice sunny day. I was lying down in the back room, resting. Out of the blue, she popped up! Clothes not matching at all. She had on pants with a skirt. The shirt didn't match, but she didn't care. All she wanted to do was play kickball with me.

When she asked, I told her, "Not right now, I'm tired."

She said, looking like a lost puppy, "Okay, Big Brother."

I replied, after looking at her, "Okay! Go in your room and get your shoes on." With the most joyful smile, she said, "Yes! Me and Big Brother!"

I instructed her to kick the ball a couple of times; then we could get some ice cream.

In the large front yard, she got her position. She started dancing in one spot, so happy to play with this big smile on her face! I rolled the ball toward her, very slowly. She kicked the ball. It went high toward the right side, hitting the house! She's laughing so hard! I said, "Girl, what are you doing? I kicked the ball straight to you." I was laughing because she was laughing. She would do this funny dance with her shoulders, going up and down, snapping her fingers. I rolled the ball again, *bop*! The ball hit the same spot. She laughed very loudly!

She said, "I'm trying, Big Brother. I'm trying!"

"I know! I know! Don't tell me! Girl, come here! Girl, no wonder you keep kicking the ball to the right. Your shoes are on the wrong feet!" I said. We laughed so much!

My lil' sister was four years old. She had this idea for us to bake a cake. "Okay," I said. She knew that if we made a cake, she could lick the bowl. We got the cake mix out of the cabinet. We started mixing the eggs, oil, butter. I leaned over and turned the oven on at 350 degrees. We put the mix in the pan. There was a knock at the door. My best friend, Al, asked if I was coming out to play basketball. I told him, "No! Right now I'm baking a cake with my lil' sister. Later I will."

I came back in the kitchen and my lil' sister had been eating the mix. She had mix all over her face! I said, "That's going to be the smallest cake! You can't eat it before you bake it!" With the look of a cake bandit, she said, "We can eat it before Mommy and Daddy get home."

"Okay!" I opened the oven but noticed that it wasn't hot. "Wow!" I said. "The pilot light is not working." I reached for some matches, but I didn't know she had turned the gas even higher. The first match blew out. The second match blew out. "Keisha, we have one match left." I struck the match, and it went, WOOSH! I turned around, looked right at her, real slowly. She burst into laughter, holding her stomach from laughing so hard. She said, "Go look in the mirror!"

I could feel my skin tingling. And my hair smelled burnt. I felt my eyelids tightening as well. I looked in the mirror. I shouted, "Keisha, "Keisha!" She started laughing again!

My eyebrows were gone! Completely burned off! GONE! My lil' sister said, "I have a magic marker! I took the magic marker in the bathroom with me. I tried to work my magic to color them in, but again, not happening! Nope! So, I took off one of my socks and stretched it around my head, just like a headband.

My dad called me out of the bathroom. I tried to keep my distance, but he asked me to come into the kitchen. He said, "What's on your head, boy?"

I said, "My Kung Fu Headband!"

He said, sniffing, "What's that smell?" Keisha was laughing still. "What smell? What's burning?"

I looked at my lil' sister with a mad look! She was whispering, "Please! Please! Don't tell on me!" I mumbled, "The oven tried to kill me!" My dad said, "WHAT?" I said, "I burned something in the oven."

She never said anything about it ever again.

Pages of Tears

The Blueprint

When Ms. Ruth and MLS' my little sister's children walked back into the waiting room, their faces were lifeless. Such an unbearable sight. I didn't even want to look at them, because I knew I would lose it! I put myself in their souls. My mother tried to hold back my tears. This is not just my lil' sister. I helped raise her, like my own daughter. She was my blueprint for raising a younger sibling. The way I cared for Keisha is the same way I care for my two sons.

I could feel every beat of my heart, just working overtime, beat after beat. As my heartbeat began to slow down, every blink became a flash of light. That flash of light became a photo flash of my lil' sister's life.

I really wanted this to be a dream, but it wasn't. It was reality. I shook my head in disbelief. "This cannot be happening to us. This cannot be happening. God, not my lil' sister! Not my lil' sister, Keisha, as tears streamed down my face.

"This cannot be happening to us," I kept telling God this over and over. Ty and I started walking toward my lil' sister's room. Every step was a nightmare. I couldn't catch my breath quick enough to even breathe correctly. I closed my eyes with fourteen steps to go. I was hoping this was all a dream. With seven steps to go, with my eyes still closed, I saw a moving white and silver shadow over my lil' sister, so I opened my eyes and let Ty walk ahead of me, thinking that if my sister fainted, I would catch her.

She's Alive!

My lil' sister was lying there, motionless and lifeless. Wait a minute! She said something. In a whisper, she said, "Take my hand, Big Brother." Her eyes slightly opened as Ty and I walked in.

"Yes, Keisha! Oh my God! You're alive! She's alive! Girl, you scared all of us! You almost didn't make it, girl."

She told me to take her hand. I noticed that one of her nails was hanging off her finger. As I held her hand, I reached for a Band-Aid to wrap around her finger. I noticed she was breathing kind of slow. Her eyes opened, just a little bit.

Ty and I stood there. She didn't say much at all.

"I love you, Keisha," I said. "Girl, I love you." That's all I kept saying, kissing her forehead and holding her cold hand. I was overwhelmed that she was talking to me.

I noticed her stomach was moving, still kind of slow. As we looked eye-to-eye, she said with a soft whisper, "Hey, Big Brother! Hey, Big Brother. I love you so much."

I kept saying, "Let me go get Ma and Pops! The doctor! You made it back, girl! You made it back, Keisha! My lil' sister made it back!" Ty just looked at me. Still crying, I couldn't believe it. I leaned down to kiss her forehead, which was slightly cold. She whispered to me, "As I lie here…" I was so overwhelmed! I took a deep breath. After my deep breath, my hearing became greater, just like at my house. I didn't have to lean over her now to hear her. I held her cold hand, and we connected eye-to-eye.

She said, "As I lie here, one by one people are starting to weep. Thanks for helping me as my soul starts to leave. Quick! Go get my family and friends!" When I opened my eyes, everyone looked surprised

"Hey family!" she called, smiling with one tear in her eye.

"How are you feeling?" we asked.

"So happy that everyone's by my side," she replied.

I couldn't stop looking at her. Her face, her hair, her lovely eyes, her lovely hands, her nails that she just had manicured. As I stroked her hair, I remembered all the times I styled her hair. I leaned over to give her a kiss. My lips touched her cold cheek. I said, "I love you, Lil' Sis, you know you'll always be my lil' sister."

She said, "I love you too, Big Brother. I love you, too." I was now in shock mode because she's talking with an "oropharyngeal down her throat. It's a curved airway that is inserted through the unconscious person's mouth into the throat to maintain a clear airway for breathing or resuscitation.

Spirit to Spirit

Ty at that moment knew something wasn't right with me. I was getting upset because no one came to my lil' sister's aid. "Someone come quick and take the tubing out of her mouth! It's hard for her to talk!" I yelled. All this time, Keisha hadn't come back to life. She had passed on. I was talking to her spirit, which passed through her forehead. Her spirit looked hazy. Along with the haziness, I saw sparkles. It looked like someone threw silver glitter in the air. The hair was sparkling as well. I thought I was dreaming, and I couldn't wake up. Her spirit just hovered over her body like a small cloud. At the time I didn't know what the cloud or smoke was that was hovering over her body and forehead. At that moment I realized that she was dead.

I was still confused about what had happened when I kissed her on the forehead. I didn't know how to use my "gift" yet. Keisha was showing me how to use it. I just didn't know it yet. That's why my sister was looking at me so strange. I was communicating spirit-to-spirit. I was so fascinated but puzzled. She couldn't communicate with Keisha's spirit like I could. I didn't want to ask her why she didn't connect with our lil' sis' spirit because I didn't know how to ask her, so I just stood there in shock.

I asked if she was okay. For some reason I felt happy but sad seeing Keisha lying there lifeless. As she lay there, I noticed her eyes were sparkling. There was one sparkling tear that wouldn't fall, as if to say, "Good-bye, Big Brother, and thank you so much for listening to me. Thank you for showing me what love is and everything about life. I'll miss you and I love you so much. Thank you, Ty, for always being there for me and my big brother. I admired you so much as a child growing up. I wanted to be just like you and Big Brother." I just couldn't let Keisha's hand go. Love wouldn't let me let it go.

My heart was crying so much. My deep voice became so soft, like a butterfly flapping its wings. Still in shock and confused, I wished I could keep her last tear from falling. Ty kept saying, "Let's go now. I'm here for you."

As I let my lil' sister's hand go, I placed them gently on her stomach. That last tear slowly ran down her cold face, just sparkling. I felt a breeze pass by me. I knew it was Keisha. I glanced back one more time before exiting her room. Again, I told her I loved her so much. I felt the tears streaming down my face now. I could hear her soft voice, "I love you, too, Big Brother. I'm okay. I'm okay." Her eyes closed as we walked away.

I kept saying, "I love her so much. I love her so much," as Ty and I walked out of Keisha's room, holding hands, I asked her, "What am I going to do now? I'll never be the same again."

I sat next to my parents. I closed my eyes, tears streaming down my face, thinking, *Why God? Why my lil' sister?*

I remember caring for her as a young girl. She always wanted to share everything. I remember all the things were shared together, like her first birthday; riding her bicycle; playing kickball; playing jacks; cards; picking flowers so she could put them in her hair; showing her how to dress; putting on makeup; being a young lady; boys, and growing up. When she graduated from high school, she was ready for the world. At least she thought she was! Her wonderful life cut short. I still don't understand. I will miss talking and laughing with her.

Is There a Heaven?

I remember a time when my mother was working. She would call and tell me to go get my lil sister from day care. The distance seemed very far, but knowing when I picked her up she would be so happy to see me, I didn't really care about the long walk. Every time I picked her up, she would come running. "Big Brother! Big Brother!" When she came out, she wanted to show me what she had done all day. She would ask me a thousand questions. She was very smart for her age. She would ask me, looking up at the sky, "Big Brother, is there a heaven up there?" I would look up at the sky too.

"It sure is a heaven," I responded.

"Yeah, but all those clouds in the sky! Where is heaven? Where's God? Where's Jesus? How do we get there? Can we go? You wanna go too? Do we take a bus or an airplane? What do I wear? Can you take me there?"

"Keisha! Keisha! Slow down," I said. "One day you'll be there."

Her Smile

Leaving my family at that moment was very hard for me, but I had to pick up my younger brother from school. On the way to the school, I remembered that Keisha was on the Pom Pom Squad in 1998. I attended several of her competitions. She was so happy to be a part of the team. I enjoyed watching my lil' sister dance and do her thing. On the stage she would blossom. Her smile made me happy.

Other students loved to be around Keisha. She had the most caring heart. Those who met her in person would be greeted with the warmest and most beautiful smile. I always told her, "A loving smile goes straight to the heart." Hers definitely did.

Before I got into my truck to pick up my younger brother, my spiritual consciousness was at a high level. As I looked around, my vision was again so acute. It amazed me.

It started to snow. One thing about the spiritual side, your way of life is altered forever. You don't see your surroundings the same way. Never! You can be afraid like I was at first, or really see beyond.

As the snow fell, I could zoom in and out, looking at every drop. I could see the crystals in the snow. In the spirit world, everything's three-dimensional. I was new to the spiritual world.

The snow was that clear to me. Have you ever heard snow hitting the ground? Of course not! Your ears aren't that sensitive. In the spiritual world, you can. I could hear snow falling, touching the ground so softly. My dad could see the snow falling as well. He would tell me later in the day about it. Looking around, people and cars were passing me. I could see the moles on their faces, if they had any. I noticed the sadness in people's eyes very quickly. I also keened in on scratches and dings on trucks and cars that passed me by. At that moment I looked straight up in the sky. Yes, the snow was falling and gently touching my face. What I saw next really fascinated me. I saw water drops that transformed into snow right before my very eyes. I didn't blink the whole time I was looking up.

At that time my soul and my spirit wanted to ask God, "Why must you take my sister now? Why? She's twenty-eight years old. All she talked about was turning thirty." God answered me, "Quest, I need her here now, my son." I didn't attend church like I should have been, however, after this experience, I attend church on a regular basis.

First I thought someone was playing a joke on me because the voice was so mild, deep and soothing, not like my own. My voice is very deep, but it was nothing like the voice that I heard in my head, so I knew it wasn't me. I stood there in sheer disbelief that God was talking to me.

I couldn't help but think about one thing: Why, out of the blue, was my little sister gone? I started crying as I asked God several times, "Why? Why? Why?" I screamed so loud, but nothing came out of my mouth!

To Keisha

You left without saying good-bye.

I still have your text in my phone, thanking me for a being such a wonderful person in your life. I knew one day you would make someone happy to be their wife.

I'm here thinking of you. Why were you taken away? Couldn't God just wait one more day? I can still see your smile. Hear your voice saying, "I love you too." I cry so much from the thought of missing you.

I think back when you were five years old, the fresh-picked flowers in your hair. I've taught you how to share and care. Without you my heart I can't bear.

If God gave me one more day with you,

I would show the world how much I love you so,

I'll tell you more and more jokes so you could laugh out loud.

You're the first baby I've ever held, so now when I look up in the clouds, I'll see your beautiful face, there smiling so proudly.

I can't help not to cry because this happened just clear out of the blue. But why me?

God has called you, so it's okay with me. The love we shared set my spirit free.

My love for you, Keisha is so deep and spiritual. We're always connected.

Mad At God

Driving home was a disaster. I thought I would never reach my destination. I wanted to yell some more! I was mad at God for taking my lil' sister away from me and my family and friends. I didn't want to accept the loss. "God, you could have taken a bird, dog or cat, but not my lil' sister," I told him. I had stopped going to church, so I thought that maybe God was punishing me. I was hoping my spiritual power would come. I wanted to see if Keisha made it to heaven. I stood there in hopes, but nothing happened. My vision was normal, along with my hearing and smell. Nothing! "Thank you, God! Thank you for the gift. What gift?" I thought that was my imagination playing tricks on me. That's what I told myself. *I'm probably in shock. Yeah, I'm in shock. It didn't happen, besides, who's going to believe me anyway? No one, they'll just think I'm crazy!*

I sat on my sofa, hoping this was all a bad dream. I called my mother's house and spoke to my dad. He said, "When I came out of the hospital, I noticed the snow falling in slow motion." Hearing him say this, I didn't respond. I thought, "There's no way he saw what I saw and my mother, brothers, and sisters didn't either." I was so amazed about this revelation because I was living through the same spiritual consciousness myself! He asked me how I was doing. I replied, "I'm still in shock, Pops. He responded, "I just spoke to her last night. She came over the house and was laughing and dancing. She was very happy. Man, I can't believe this, I just can't!" What I did notice and feel from my dad was love. Love he had for Keisha. Keisha and my dad shared a close bond. Dad had this secret that he really didn't talk about at all. He was an all-star basketball player. All his peers thought he was one of the coolest guys. He didn't want anyone thinking he wasn't cool, so he didn't tell anyone about his gift for twenty-five years. It was a huge shock, but I knew in my heart and deep in my spirit that he was telling the truth. My dad was spiritual. That was his secret for all these years. He also was very creative. My dad taught us how to use our creative eye, showing us that we can see things from our surroundings that people couldn't see or fathom. We all could just stare at something, like a tree, ring, leaf—anything. We all saw the same thing. Keisha could see things very fast. She would tell my dad things he couldn't see.

We all would stare at a stain and see which one would come up with a face or picture first. Sometimes it would be me, Ty, or Keisha.

As we said our good-byes over the phone, I tried to relax and just calm down. I heard a voice, "Just take some deep breaths and just relax. Relax, Big Brother."

I shouted, "Keisha, is that you?" No response. I knew it was a girl's voice. I couldn't relax after what I had heard. That night it was hard for me to go to sleep. I called a girlfriend over to watch me sleep. She couldn't make it because she had kids of her own to look after. That night I didn't go to sleep. I couldn't sleep. My mind was feeling overwhelmed. I couldn't even think straight! As I drifted off, I felt I was being watched. I started to hear real quiet voices. *My mind must be playing tricks on me again*, I thought. Still no sleep for two days!

On Friday, I asked my girlfriend to come watch me sleep. This night I was very tired. I thanked her for coming and looking over me that night. I sat on the end of my bed. I almost started crying, but I held myself together. I started thinking about my lil' sis, how she was doing. Was she okay? Was she safe? I said, "Keisha, give me a sign that you're okay." A minute passed, and there was no sign. Then it happened.

My air vent was completely closed. It just opened up by itself. My girlfriend said, "Okay, tell me your air vent didn't just open by itself!"

I said, "You're not going to believe me, but that was my little sister telling me she's okay."

I wanted to tell her everything that happened to me. Then I thought, *She wouldn't believe me anyway*. Some people can't fathom what I experienced and heard. My dreams that night weren't dreams anymore. I started having spiritual dreams, but these dreams were not like other dreams that I had experienced in the past. They were vivid with brilliant colors. All I kept hearing in my dreams were voices: male and female voices telling me to believe in my spiritual connections and have faith. I awoke to voices, chimes, my little sister laughing, people clapping, Cheers, music, and then it happened.

I heard my sister's voice, "Big Brother!"

I got up thinking my sons had left the patio doors open. As I walked toward the patio doors, I reached for something to protect myself, thinking someone had broken into my house. I heard several men's voices. I had a house alarm, but it didn't alert me. All the voices and noises did. It was like they were partying out on my patio! I stepped closer but noticed the voices and sounds drifting away from the patio. I went outside to check the surroundings but found nothing suspicious. I re-entered my house, making sure I locked everything. I returned to my bedroom, not thinking anything of it. I put my hands behind my head.

"Hey, Big Brother!"

It was my lil' sister's voice. I thought I was dreaming, but her voice sounded so clear through all of that cheering.

My Little Sister Talking

I shouted, "Keisha! Is that you? Keisha! Keisha!"

As I ran to my patio, I noticed my chimes on the patio weren't moving, but I could hear them. The wind wasn't blowing at all. The voice didn't drift this time. I could hear them loud and clear. I just couldn't make out my sister's voice because her voice was so faint. I sat down at my table near my living room and patio, just in case I heard it again.

I asked my lil' sister to come to me and help me finish her second book. The first one, *Who I Am*, was already a hit. At this time, sitting there calmly and ready for her, I heard voices and music again. This time I wasn't moving. I turned, looking over my shoulder.

"Hey, Big Brother!"

"Keisha, is that you?"

"Yeah! It's me, Big Brother!"

I turned back around because now my heart was beating so fast. My law enforcement training prepared me not to be afraid, but calm. This was different. I said, "I can't really hear you, Keisha. You're not that clear."

Within three seconds, I heard a sound like air coming out of a bottle.

"Hey, Big Brother! How's that?" she asked in a sparkling clear voice.

I jumped up, gasping for air! I burst into tears and continued crying. With my hands covering my face, I could hear her voice, sparkling clear. My emotions got the best of me. I ran to my room because I was so scared!

"Big Brother, please calm down."

"This can't be real. This can't be real," I said. "Oh, my God! I can't believe this!"

"Oh, don't say 'can't'. You have to take a couple of deep breaths for me. I know this is shocking to you, but this is real. You can see me if you calm down and take a deep breath. Believe! Believe! All you have to do is believe in me. God sent me for you. We want to show you heaven."

"God sent you? Did I die? Am I dead?" I started crying harder, almost having a panic attack. "Why did you leave me? Why, Keisha? Why? You're so young. How can I live without you, Keisha?"

"It's okay, Big Brother."

"No, it's not! I love you so much, Keisha. Love you, love you!"

"Listen, I need you to calm down, right now!"

My tears slowed down as I calmed down.

"That's it, Big Brother. You don't have to cry anymore. I'm okay."

As my emotions settled, I started to see radiant stars. I opened my eyes again, unsure what I had just seen. Wow! My lil' sister's whole body was covered in beautiful stars—green, purple, white, silver, yellow, and gold. Her face was golden. I started to calm down but was still in shock. As she reached out to touch me, I jumped back, thinking it's going to hurt if she touched me! Her hands began to touch my face, ever so softly. "It's okay, Big Brother. I'm not here to hurt you. Remember that time I was five years old and we talked about going to heaven?"

"Yeah." I was crying so loudly I thought my sons were going to wake up. I couldn't stop shaking and crying.

"Big Brother, calm down! Just believe."

"I just can't help it, Keisha. I don't want you to go. Please don't go, Keisha," I pleaded.

"I'm already gone, Big Brother."

Crying, I opened my eyes to see if my sons were awake.

"They're not going to wake up until we are done. God has things under control. He really wants you to see heaven. It will be you who will tell people what you saw."

"How will I remember everything?"

"You will! You have a gift that God gave you. You just haven't believed in yourself all this time. The angels are waiting to guide you around heaven too."

"Angels? Real angels? Why me?"

"Yeah! Go over to the wall where the poster frames are resting."

"How did you know I had picture frames against my wall?" Every blink I took, I could see my lil' sister's face and body so clearly. I was still very afraid, and she knew it, telling me to calm down and believe.

"Why me, Keisha, of all people? Keisha, why me?"

"God knows you're special. All these years you've been in denial about your spiritual connections. So now, today, you're going to connect with the angels. Relax, It'll be okay. Just think. All this time you didn't know you had a gift? I knew you did, Big Brother."

"How can I relax when you're talking about angels and going to heaven? Plus, I'm talking to a ghost!"

"I'm not a ghost," she said, laughing.

I started laughing myself because she was laughing.

"I'm not here to haunt you, dummy! I want to show you where I'm at. Now look through your picture frame."

I looked through each frame.

"Not that one. Not that one. Oh my!"

"This picture frame had a swimsuit model."

"Not that one! Nice car! Nice trees. Nope! Nope! Yes! Yes! This one! This is where I am now, in the paradise picture."

"Right now? You're here with me!"

"I can travel at the speed of light."

"Yeah, right, Keisha!"

"Really, if you believe! I can take you. Do you believe?"

"Yeah, I believe. I'm talking to you, so I believe!"

"Do you really? Turn the picture sideways."

"How did you know the picture was sideways?"

"I'm looking through your eyes."

"My eyes?"

"Yeah. I can see things three-dimensional with eyes of the spirit. We share that trait, remember?"

"I knew you could. That's why I was calling you. I knew you could hear and see me."

"Yeah! How did you know that?"

"I've always had the spiritual awareness and I can be anywhere in the world at any time. You can see things other people can't see. Like me talking to you at the hospital. Ty blocked me out, but you could hear and communicate with me. That's probably why you felt a breeze. That was me passing through you."

"I thought I was imagining that when I was talking to you, and I saw sparkling stars, too. I thought I was dreaming."

"No! That was real. But afterwards, you didn't believe it was me. So I floated around. I've been flying around until you became open. With your spirit, the deep breaths you were taking helped."

"So, it was you who opened my air vent?"

"That was me! Did I scare you?"

"No. Can you teach me what I need to learn about your gifts?"

"I sure can. That's why I'm here with you right now, Big Brother. And the angels will teach you too."

"Really? Okay, I'm sorry. What's up with this picture of paradise?"

"That's where I'm at now."

The picture showed several palm trees, white sand, crystal clear ocean water, lovely clouds, and two doves flying in the air. Paradise!

"Look carefully. Look, I'm in the middle: that dot."

"Oh, I see it!"

"That's another dove. The dot is the dove's eyes."

"I never noticed it before because it blends in with the clouds."

"Right, it does. But, that's me! The other two are Ty and you. Sit down for this one. Watch the dove. Believe in yourself, take a deep breath, now four more deep breaths."

Paradise

I could feel my spiritual realm opening. I could smell the soil in my potted plant. For every deep breath I took, I could feel a breeze through my shirt.

"Open your spiritual eyes and believe, Big Brother."

As I looked at MLS my little sister, she looked normal in the human form but covered in a mist of stars. As my spiritual eyes opened, my body felt like I lost a hundred pounds. I felt like I was on a moon bounce. As I stood up and walked over to MLS my little sister, we started laughing, just like she was five years old again. I asked her, "Why you laughing?"

She said, "Look behind you!"

I looked with a slow turn. "Wow! He looks like me!"

She said, "That's you, crying at the table."

"But, if that's me, how can I be with you?" I asked."

"You're having an out-of-body experience. Your spirit is free."

"Wow! Can I fly?" I asked.

"You can fly and do other amazing things," she replied. As I looked with my earth eyes closed, tears were flowing down my face.

"Now, look at the dove."

The dove in the picture's wings started flapping. I looked with bewilderment on my face but remained calm. I opened my earth eyes again and could still see the dove flapping its wings. As my tears subsided, I began to feel very calm.

"Close your eyes," Keisha said.

"How am I going to explain this to anyone? They're gonna think I'm crazy!" As I got deeper into the realm, I saw myself sitting at the table with my eyes closed and my arms down by my side. "How can I see myself? Did I die?"

"No! This is how you get to heaven. We are doves. That other dove is you on my right side. And the other one is Ty." I really couldn't see anything except this brilliant light.

I noticed a sparkling mist with MLS, my little sister. I just thought that was part of her spiritual form. As I was told later, that was me looking at myself. That's why I felt so light. To look at myself was incredible. Shocking at first, but so blissful. I could see my every move, and my earth body couldn't see me.

"People are going to think I'm crazy, Keisha!"

"No they're not! It's okay, Big Brother."

Just like that, she passed through the ceiling as I stood there in disbelief. I took another look at myself at the table.

"Come on, Big Brother," she coaxed in a really faint voice. "Believe! Believe!"

I looked up at the ceiling and noticed it was getting closer to me. I suddenly realized I was getting closer to the ceiling!

"Come on, you can do it, Big Brother!"

I closed my eyes, spread my arms out, and started rising toward the ceiling. I opened my eyes just before my head touched the ceiling. Then, *whoosh*! All I saw was white with brilliant colors I haven't seen before.

"Follow my voice, Big Brother."

As I flew toward my lil' sister's voice, I was really enjoying all the colors, and then everything turned white! A vivid white with a baby blue background. I caught up with my lil' sister. "Wow! That was incredible! Are we in heaven?"

Paradise Island

We Ty, Keisha and I started flying toward this bright, crystal-like light. I could feel my spirit being pulled toward this light. I felt this loving feeling drawing me closer. I saw my sister sister Ty fly through first. Ty fly through first. Then I followed her. My lil' sister came through last. We were in paradise, flying through the most beautiful palm trees. You could smell the coconuts, bananas, and pineapples. "This place must be heaven, Keisha!"

"Nope. This is where you come to fly with family; be with your loved ones. The three of us to enjoy all the memories; to love each other one last time before I go to heaven."

"Why us? Why not Mom and Dad?"

"God told me to come get you."

"Yeah, but Ty is here, too.

"You started to believe more and you went and got her. I didn't."

"I could see my sister's face in place of the dove's face. "Can Ty hear me? Are we doves? How are we doves?"

"Just enjoy the moment, silly. Ty can hear you, not me."

"Why not?

"Your spirit is connected to me."

"Really?" All three of us are flying over the clear sparkling, crystal water. I could feel the sunbeam on my wings and the smell of fruit in the air. So breathtaking to look down and see tropical fish, dancing dolphins swimming with your shadows. I felt this energy of love from them. Even the waves had a connection with us. "I love it, Keisha!"

"I love you, too, Big Brother."

We continued to fly through the beautiful palm trees with the smell of fruit in the air. I looked over to both sisters as they continued to fly in harmony, wings flapping as one grace. It was wonderful, in flight, enjoying God's air. The look on Ty's face was blissful. Nothing more perfect. Nothing like watching my sisters flying together. At that moment my lil' sister told me, "When the spirit leaves the body of someone who has passed over to the other side, it hovers over that person. I could see myself lying there motionless and lifeless. I didn't know I had passed away. It happened so suddenly. I hadn't even said hello, good-bye, or I love you yet. I'm still in shock, but glad to have my brother and sister to share this journey with me. When my spirit left the hospital, I came outside with all of you." Ty was in awe and speechless.

As we stood there talking, I didn't know who to ride with! But I realized I can go with everyone! This is all new to me. I can be here and there at the blink of an eye. When I was walking on earth in the flesh, I was also sitting in the van with Mom and Dad on the way to Dad's house. I went back to my house and started thinking about all the good and bad memories I had in that house. I came to you, Big Brother, because we talked about heaven so many times when I was a child. Now, we're here flying over paradise. I asked God if I could bring you because you tried to tell me how heaven looked. God said, "Keisha, go get Quest. He's special, and I don't think he knows his spiritual ability. And you're here right now."

Keisha, while flying higher than Ty and me, started doing figure eights in the sky. It was beautiful to watch her flying so free. No pain. No worries. She used to always help people and never helped herself.

Tricks in the Air

Keisha looked so peaceful, such a gorgeous smile on her face. I couldn't help but smile at her. With her, I felt like she was five again. So much fun and freedom! I tried to do my figure eights, but my wings felt unable to do tricks in the air. It wasn't funny, I told her. If wasn't careful she could break her wings! She continued doing tricks in the air that Ty and I couldn't do. Ty was flying normally, nothing fancy or creative. I wanted to enjoy everything with my lil' sister. So, I tried to do the figure eights again. I almost fell out of the sky! My lil' sister laughed so much as I was falling, she yelled, "Believe!" As I believed, I started flying normally again, flapping my wings, which were really heavy, trying to catch up to my sisters. I finally caught up to them. My lil' sister said with a giggle, "Next time listen to me, Big Brother!"

As we flew through the palm trees, the air was pure. You could smell everything around you: bananas, pineapple and coconuts. The island sand looked soft like it had crystals in it. Over the palm trees, we all flapped our wings as one, back and forth, up and down. We were flying as one dove, so spiritual. It was love. Love we had for each other.

It was fascinating to see and touch my loved one, Keisha, after she'd passed over and to have an out-of-body experience.

"Big Brother," my lil' sister shouted.

"Yeah!" I couldn't hear because the heavenly breeze was beneath me as I flapped my wings.

"Hey! You wanna see something amazing?"

"This is amazing," I said, while enjoying flying through the soft clouds, angel clouds.

"Look! Down!"

"No way!" "Am I seeing what I think I'm seeing?"

"Yes, yes you are," as she smiled so sweetly.

"How is that possible?" As we flew above the crystal clear water, not only were the dolphins dancing with us, but they were dancing with our reflection in human form as normal shadows.

Ty's reflection showed her wearing this brilliant dress. No fashion designer could make this dress. It sparkled as if it were alive. Diamonds trimmed the dress.

Angel Clouds

I was wearing this white suit with diamonds as my tie, with diamond buttons and sun shades with crystal frames.

My lil' sis was flying higher and doing more tricks in the air.

"Beautiful!" By now we all flew through so many clouds. Wow! Look at that! We were flying through all the clouds that looked like angels!

"Hey, you smell that?" I've smelled that same smell before. I thought it was me, but it wasn't.

"But it's not!"

"We're flying in angel clouds."

"Yeah, clouds that look like angels. They smell like sugar cookies," she said.

"Sugar cookies!"

"We're very close."

"Close to what?"

"Heaven."

I became very nervous, and my feathers started falling out.

"Stay calm! It's okay, Big Brother, stay calm!"

"How high are we?"

"Very high."

I tried to keep up, but I started to tire out. I flapped and I flapped my wings, so close, about an inch away from her wings. I flapped again very hard. Now we're even, flying as one again. Ty wasn't flying at this height. She continued to fly at a lower height under the angel clouds. I could see her just enjoying the heavenly breezes. Keisha closed her wings and put her head down and went straight down like a plane, nose diving, then shot straight up like a rocket, flying right past me! Wow! Now that's a trick! But, I noticed there wasn't a reflection of her over the water. "Keisha!" I yelled.

"Yeah, Big Brother?"

"Okay, where's your reflection on the water?"

"That's what I've been trying to tell you! I don't have one!"

"Yeah right! What trick is that? That's amazing, girl! How do you do that?"

"No! It's not your time, Big Brother. It's almost time for me to go, flying higher.

This time I could not keep up with her. "Wait up, Keisha!"

"God is calling me now. I have to go meet my angels."

"Angels? God?"

"I love you. I'll see you again" she said to Ty.

"What do you mean you'll see her soon?" I asked as I got an inch from her wings again.

This time she looked over at m. "I love you, Big Brother."

"I love you, too," I replied as I flapped my wings harder but I just couldn't go that high.

"Big Brother, you can't fly this high. It's not your time. I love you!" she said as she smiled at me. I love you. Tell Mom and Dad I love them from the bottom of my heart. I'll see them one day in heaven."

I flapped my wings as hard and as fast as I could, catching up right behind her, one feather inch!

"Keisha," I yelled.

"Big Brother, take a deep breath! Close your eyes! Now open them," she instructed me.

She was gone! All I saw was white! I started to cry! I felt so left behind. So alone. I could see Ty still flying around under angel clouds, so peacefully, just enjoying the fresh air under her wings. Then I heard my lil' sister's voice.

Welcome Her Back

So clean! Her smile! So welcoming! When she turned around, she still had her wings on her back. She looked at me and said, "Don't stop believing." My senses came alive when she told me that I could now see three dimensions, like I could now see at my house. To see yourself like this, and everything around you, it's unbelievable! Eyes of the spirit world see more dimensions than earthly eyes of the mortal body. I can see in all directions at once. When I had my first out-of-body experience, I didn't recognize myself. I stood right beside my lil' sister. I couldn't stop hugging her. We started walking toward the shining object, but it didn't feel like we were walking. It felt like we were walking and floating at the same time. I felt weightless. As we got closer, this object became larger. This object was fifty feet long and twelve feet high. My lil' sister and I just stood there smiling at each other.

We started smelling cookies again. As we looked around, no one was there. I looked back at her and asked, "What's this? Where are we?"

We Entered Heaven

The smell really became stronger. We didn't know what to expect. The object began to vibrate and was floating in mid air. Floating!

I told my lil' sister, "It looks like a giant flat screen. A 50 foot flatscreen!"

We started laughing, not knowing what this was. As I stepped forward to touch it, the object moved backwards. My lil' sister, laughing, stepped forward, then took another step. The object didn't move, but I noticed Keisha's' wings on her back weren't moving either. The smell of sugar cookies faded away. My lil' sister touched the screen and it turned on.

"This has to be a TV," I said.

With a serious face, Keisha said, "It's not!"

"So, what is it?" I inquired. "It's a mirror," Keisha said. "What do you mean it's a mirror? Not that big, Keisha!"

Keisha opened her hand, fingers stretched out and placed it on the screen. The object turned into a mirror right before my eyes!

"What? How could it? No way, Keisha, no way! I've never seen a mirror this large before." That's all I kept saying over and over. My hearing was at a higher level at this moment than before. I started hearing a baby cry. I kept saying, "I've heard that cry before."

"Of course you have; that's me!" Keisha told me.

I said, "What do you mean it's you?"

The mirror started flashing so rapidly that earth eyes would not be able to catch every flash. In the spirit world we could. It looked like a flash, but in fact, it was my lil' sister as a baby. All her baby life moments, from the time she was born, just getting her first breath of earth's air. Astounding!

As I stood there with her, we started laughing. I saw the first time I fed her, changed her, bathed her, brushed her hair. Such great memories. As the flashes slowed down, the mirror started showing every moment of her life. At that time we glanced at each other, holding her hand, tightly, and at the same time we said, "The mirror of life!"

To see my lil' sister at age two through five years old made me want to cry. I could feel myself crying on earth. I was so amazed at the "Mirror of Life." I felt breathless for several minutes, looking at every moment of her life.

The mirror flashed back to when we were in the hospital and Keisha's spirit leaving her body through her head, right before I gave her my last kiss. Her spirit touched my face. Looking at my sister, Ty I could see that she and Keisha were looking at each other face-to-face. Keisha's spirit hovered over her body, transforming into a "dove-like" form. From that point on the "Mirror of Live" displayed the three of us flying over earth clouds, angel clouds and all the way to Keisha and I standing in front of the "Mirror of Life." All of it was like watching a side show. Above the mirror was a purple cloud that transformed into a lot of letters. It read: "The Mirror of Life," in purple lettering! The clouds turning into a large ribbon, like platinum silver. Just lovely! We started smelling sugar cookies and smoke. The smell at first was very faint. The smoke was like something burning, like burnt cookies, but not overly burnt. The "Heaven Clouds" started dancing again.

On earth the clouds look plain and simple. The clouds are just moving. In heaven they "dance." We saw the clouds turn colors, from white to silver; silver to purple; purple to a brilliant yellow. All the clouds sparkled with joy. As the smell of sugar cookies became stronger, we saw another cloud that danced right in front of us. We noticed this one particular sparkling cloud. As it came closer, the cloud started transforming. We first noticed these shimmering pants, which emerged from the clouds, silky like! It looked like the pants were stuffed with clouds, just dancing. They were the silkiest pants we have ever seen. You couldn't buy these pants anywhere. They were white in color with diamond-like stones on them.

Then another pair of pants came into view. This time they were a soft green, almost hazel/silver. Then it happened! The clouds faded away. Two people appeared; one male and one female with clouds circling their chest and waist area. They were silver. They walked toward us. I stood in front of Keisha like a Big Brother's instincts would do. These weren't just creatures from earth, their faces were platinum and blurry, as if they were made out of these brilliant stars! As they walked closer toward us, their faces became clearer, but I noticed the male face. It looked transgendered. They both looked transgendered and had this perfect look: different, but pretty/very handsome. They stood there staring at us. I'm still in awe at what they were wearing: silky night-time attire, close to transparent silver in color.

Their wings opened up. I thought my lil' sister's wings were a nice size. Their wings were incredible! They started to glow, from their face down to their perfect hands. The male angel's wings were about 8 ft. long. The female's wings were about six feet long, straight out. I'm in shock from the size of their wings. Shock, but amazement! I had to take a deep breath! They were right in front of us, smelling like sugar cookies. I looked down at my feet. I don't know why I did that, but I couldn't see myself. I saw my lil' sister's feet. I was now lost. Lost in my spirit, from shock. My sister said, "No! No you're not! You started crying back on earth. But, it's okay, Big Brother." My mind and heart were in shock. "Stop crying and breathe!," she demanded. I could see myself sitting at the table in my house, still crying. I was amazed I could see myself. How? How could I see myself, so many miles away, so quickly? A blink of an eye! Amazing, but true! Heaven Heaven speed!

I finally stopped crying and began to focus again, getting control of my breathing again. My mind began focusing on getting back to heaven. My body looked like a human shell. My eyes were opened. It's like I'm in a trance, blinking very slowly.

I came back to heaven in a speed of light, standing next to my lil' sister, as if I hadn't left.

The angels said, "mmmmm." I couldn't help but ask questions. "Maybe it's me, but y'all smell like sugar cookies, some good sugar cookies! You're making me hungry!" My lil' sister started to laugh, shaking her head! The angels turned and looked at me and started laughing! I said, "Wow, angels laugh!" They spoke in unison, "We sure do!" I really felt the love emanating from them. I could not explain the feeling, but it felt so good! I kept getting that butterfly feeling in my stomach. For every step the angels took toward us, I became more in love, all my thoughts were positive. I wanted to love everyone. My love for people deepened. I wanted to give my love to all. As I kept looking into their eyes, my heart was pumping love all throughout my body. The wind started to blow and I noticed their wings were picture-perfect! Their wings had me in a trance! The more they stretched out, the more I felt the love from them. As they got closer, the smell of sugar cookies filled the air around us. They moved and turned their heads at the same time.

My lil' sister's angel began to speak. "Hello, K. Yvonne. How are you doing? Did you enjoy your 'Mirror of Life' experience? We are here to guide you and help you. If you have any questions, feel free to ask us, K. Yvonne."

"Can they see me?" I asked my lil' sister because I couldn't see myself!

They turned in unison and said, "We can see you, Quest," ending their sentence in harmony.

I noticed that as they got closer, I could hear music, so I asked, "Where is the music coming from?"

"It is us, Quest, that you hear music radiating from."

What "Quest" Means

The clouds made their own music every time the wind blew. I said, "It sounds like chimes." The angels responded, "You're right, Quest."

"We have questions for you."

"Yes," I said. "Do you know what your name means?"

I said, "Yes, the special one who was touched by heaven's light." They smiled and said, "Yes, on earth, Quest. In heaven your name means 'The special one who was kissed by a rose in heaven. The special one who touched the kingdom's doors.' It is you who will teach people to believe in themselves, Quest, and lead them to God's glory light."

"Wow! Who is going to believe me when I tell them this?" I asked.

"Do you not believe what you have seen? Do you not believe what you have touched, Quest? We are angels from God's glory." We looked at each other, eye-to-eye. No one blinked.

As my glance deepened, I said, "I do believe. This is real! I'm standing here with you, two angels from God's light. Please touch me." We all held hands and closed our eyes. I felt so loved at that moment.

Everyone in heaven loves each other. I could feel love from everyone who walked past me. I felt joy and happiness all day long. If someone walked past you and said, "I love you" and hugged you, would you be offended? In heaven that's how it was. I saw people telling others just that! Love: that's what the world needs: to love each other. Tell someone you love them from the bottom of your heart. Say it with a smile. That might change their whole day.

Yes! I was amazed, but more amazed because the whole time we're communicating their mouths never moved. We had been communicating telepathically. They told me my spiritual level was brilliant for someone who hasn't passed over yet. But this journey was all about my lil' sister bringing me to heaven because we used to talk about heaven when she was a young child. So they brought me there with them to enjoy their journey.

The angels touched my lil' sister's wings, touching them softly and gently. Her wings settled down. We all took fourteen steps toward this artistic water fountain. This statue looked so real. Keisha and I were astounded. We were grinning and laughing from our amazement. This statue was of a large hand. God's hand, with angels all around. The angels were pouring water on God's hands.

We took one blink; then there were two hands, so life-like. Just amazing! The voices in my head kept telling me that these were God's hands, so soft but very large. The perfect fingerprints. As I looked closer, his prints were in forms of letters. "L.O.V.E"! I took a double take, shaking my head in awe. "Love."

Touching these hands made me think about people in the world who need love, who need someone to care for them. I felt so at peace. To see angels pouring water in His hands was wonderful. As God's hands moved slowly, together, like God wanted us to drink out of His hands, the water poured down slowly, splashing, while the water continued to pour under his hands. Again, such nice music, almost like jazz, a smooth jazz! With all the angels around me, it seemed as though the fountain was playing music. The water looked like liquid diamonds. My lil' sister ran her hands through the water, so pure.

There was no water on her hands at all. She did this several times as the angels looked on. They said, "K. Yvonne, you only drink the water to purify your spirit, nothing more."

I asked, "Can I drink some?"

"Only K. Yvonne and people who have crossed over can drink this water, Quest. It will only taste like water to you," they responded.

My little sister ran her hands through again. Nothing on her hands! She leaned down and took a sip of the water. I could see the water going down her throat, going through her body. I asked, "What just happened to my lil' sister? Why did the water do that to her body?"

The angels said, "Her spirit is purified with heaven's water. One sip is all you need to drink, Quest."

"Yeah, but the water looked clear. How did it turn blue?" I questioned.

"She's giving her spirit to God, That's why it went down blue, Quest."

I wanted to be a part of this heavenly experience. I took a sip while the angels watched. I couldn't let my lil' sister do this alone. The water didn't turn blue for me. Sip after sip, nothing happened. I was very disappointed.

"You can continue with us, Quest. We see the spiritual love you have for K. Yvonne."

We looked to our right and noticed friends and family and celebrities! Everywhere! They came from the clouds or maybe from God's hands. I'm still in such amazement from my experience. People everywhere! I didn't notice anyone, because I was looking at my lil' sister's face. I asked, "What's wrong?"

She said, "Oh my! Oh my!" with a big smile on her face. "Marvin Gaye! Marvin Gaye, Big Brother!"

"Yeah, right," I said is disbelief. As I looked, I was in awe "Dad's not going to believe this, Keisha!"

"I can't believe Marvin Gaye just walked in front of me," she shouted!

"Marvin! Marvin! My mom and dad, me, my Big Brother, love you, man!"

The angels spoke, this time moving their mouths, "K. Yvonne, you don' have to yell," speaking softly to my lil' sister. "We know you're excited, K. Yvonne, but you can just whisper. He can hear you from just a whisper."

"Hey, Marvin," she said in a whisper, "I love you!"

Marvin looked at us and said, "I love you too. Welcome!"

In awe, I said, "Did Marvin just speak to us?"

"Yes, Quest. He's a wonderful person," replied the angels.

Paradise Wings

The angels turned Keisha around to adjust her wings.

"K. Yvonne, or Keisha? Let's take your wings off and put them over here." They put them in a blue box. The box was three feet long with clouds in it as cushioning. The angels said, "If you ever want to go fly around paradise, we'll give these back to you. These are paradise wings, so you can do tricks in the air."

"So, are they trick wings, because she was doing some tricks with them?" I asked. "You hear me!" That was the second time I heard the angels laugh. "I noticed that when you "flolk," it's so peaceful." I'm trying to explain as best I can, but it isn't easy, as to what a "flolk" is. However, if you walk with your loved one, down a sidewalk and you stop, but your loved one keeps walking, just a blink and you'll be right beside them. No running, just walking and floating at the same time. Never on earth, just in heaven only.

My lil sister and I started smelling the most pleasant smell. So clean. It just made me think of Febreeze, but cleaner. We also could hear wings flapping. We looked up and saw butterflies.

They were more beautiful than earth butterflies. Larger, almost like a small bird. Purple and silver ones, red and yellow, green and pure white. These butterflies actually communicated with us. What made this so special, they were in 3-D! So amazing!

I remember on earth a butterfly landed on my forearm. It's rare for a butterfly to touch a human in open space. It landed on my forearm, just relaxing. Its wings were still, just relaxing. It was a very special moment for me, as if we were communicating.

In heaven, they fly to you, right in front of your face, looking eye-to-eye. Their wings flap so softly, it was musical. When the butterflies fly near the angels, it sounds so relaxing and loving. The music that came from their wings made you want to love someone. I was loving my lil' sister and heaven, the whole time. We held hands, just like she was five years old again. This brought back so many memories of my lil' sister and I. I used to sit out front of the house and watch her admire the butterflies. And, now they were right in front of us, looking eye-to-eye. We could see ourselves in their eyes. Just mind-blowing! I could see hundreds of them, their wings making music, like someone playing the violin, real softly. We stood there enjoying the music from the angels, butterflies and the clouds. The best smooth jazz music ever heard! I can't find an earth word to describe it!

The butterflies began to transform into angels. Everywhere! "Do you see that, Keisha? Wow!" The most brilliant colors. We stood there taking everything in, I didn't know how I was going to remember all of this. It's like your best Christmas ever, only a trillion times better! Like going to Disney World, only a trillion times better! You don't know what to expect. Unreal on earth because you can't fathom it! But I'm here with my lil' sister, walking with two angels. To see the others transform was priceless!

I'm telling you everything up here has music deep within them. I've heard it. I got so excited to touch so many angels. I can't recall how many I touched, but it felt wonderful. I put my arms out straight, took a deep breath and relaxed, letting the butterflies fly all around me. "I love this!" I said to Keisha. "I love you for bringing me here, lil' sister!"

They all just looked at me with the same look in their eyes. I noticed the clouds changing colors.

All my lil' sis and I could see were clouds. It started getting foggy, but those were just clouds around us. The clouds turned blue to gray to white to pure white. Then the clouds started glowing super bright.

On earth it's like looking at the sun at its hottest peak. You can't look straight at it. In heaven, in the spiritual world, you can. It was bright, but we didn't blink or squint. We "flolked" toward the light. Squeezing my lil' sister's hand tighter, very firm, as we "flolked" closer. It was welcoming. We felt love at every step we took, causing us to gasp for air!

The angels spoke, "You can relax. Relax! Get ready."

We didn't know what to expect next.

I could feel myself on earth, starting to cry because I thought my lil' sister was leaving me at that moment. She kept saying, "It's okay, Big Brother! Don't cry!" I left my little sister right there and went back to earth, where I saw myself at the table crying so hard. I was in shock as I sat at the table crying. I noticed that I'd been crying so much my shirt was drenched with tears.

I knew the time was getting nearer to say good-bye to my lil' sister. I was enjoying this moment in heaven. I didn't want to come back home to earth!

I hovered over myself at the table. As I looked up and around I saw a dazzling mist hovering over me. I could see myself shaking and crying. I wanted to cry, but you don't cry in heaven. There's nothing but joy and happiness.

I told myself, "Quest, it's me, your spirit. I need you to calm down."

I, earth Quest, said, "How can I calm down when I just lost my lil' sister?"

Earth Quest stood up again, my shirt drenched with tears. I, Spirit Quest, walked right up to Earth Quest. There's nothing like seeing yourself out-of-body, walking and talking, just the whole out-of-body experience. I said, "Calm down," touching my own face. "Calm down. I love you. I love you." Those three words completely calmed me down. I sat back down and started taking deep breaths for myself. As Earth Quest became calmer, I left my body and returned to heaven.

Back in heaven: It was as though I paused a movie. We continued to "flolk" toward the heaven's light. The angels asked me, "Are you okay, Quest?"

"Yes, why do you ask?" I inquired.

"There's a tear in your eye," they responded.

"Really?" My "Earth Quest" was crying at that moment, and the angels reached their hands out like stop motions toward me, then turned their hands around with an open palm. I saw rain drops falling toward their palms, touching and disappearing. "Is it raining?" I asked.

"No, these are your tears. You're fine now, Quest," they explained.

My lil' sister looked at me and said, "They must really love you!"

Turning around we could see the light directly in front of us. The female angel went through the light first, stating, "It's okay. You're here at the palace." I went through next, but noticed my clothes had changed. I had a white and yellow outfit on.

"How did I change so fast?" I inquired.

"You didn't. You never once looked at your outfit the whole time you've been here, Quest," they told me with a smile!

"Really?"

"Really, Quest," they responded.

My lil' sister walked through and gasped for air. "This is how heaven looks, Big Brother!" she explained excitedly. The male angel followed, "Yes, K.Yvonne," they concurred. I couldn't see anything because "Earth Quest" had started crying again, blocking my visions.

Both angels put their palms out again. As the tears came forward, my vision began to improve. White lights were everywhere. The angels instructed us to blink two times.

I blinked once, then twice. The light that was so bright was a reflection of the palace. We all "flolked" toward the palace and again butterflies and doves appeared everywhere the eye could see. The sky was a special color blue. It made you feel loved. Nothing on earth was this color.

Palm trees! Yeah palm trees! I could smell them! But, the palace smelled like a "rhythm of fruits." Every fruit in the world was here. Butterflies kept flying over the palace, landing on the rooftop. The sidewalls were so high with very large windows. There was gold trimming around the top of the palace. The walls were shimmering and sparkling. The butterflies transformed into angels. Music was playing everywhere! Love was in the air. Heaven made you love one another instantly.

Roses That Love

As we "flolked" toward the gleaming palace, we noticed roses in brilliant colors. These weren't just any roses. The stems were hazel and shimmered. If you were to take glitter and sprinkle just a pinch over the roses, they would change colors right in front of you. I bent down to touch one of the roses.

"Wow! Did you see that, Sis?" I asked.

"Yeah!" she exclaimed with a laugh. "That's beautiful. The rose turned colors right in front of our faces."

As I looked closer, I could hear the heartbeat from the rose. I looked at the angels and said, "Wow! Tell me that just didn't happen!"

The angels explained, "Yes, Quest, it did. If your heart has love, they will love you too!"

"Wow! The most beautiful flowers just bloomed right in front of my eyes!" At first glance I noticed the greenest grass. As I continued to look, I noticed stems that were dancing back and forth, just growing, then *pop*! The flowers just popped out and bloomed, opened up! The most sparkling pink that shot out white and silver glitter.

"Quest, that's not glitter," the angels told me.

"It's not?"

"No, Quest! It's love seeds. The flowers are saying they love you, Quest."

"What are love seeds?" I questioned.

"You see how the grass is that green? The flowers get happy to be in love with a new spirit. As you are the new spirit, the grass feeds off those seeds," the angels clarified. I wanted to eat the flowers because they smelled like cotton candy. When I touched them they turned purple! So beautiful!

"The flowers love me? How about the roses?" I asked. They told me that the roses did love me. The rose opened its petals. I could see inside. These roses weren't just beautiful; they were intelligent! They bowed their heads when I walked up on them. The rose that I fell in love with was loving me as well. As I leaned to smell it, the rose softly kissed my face.

That kiss felt like an earth kiss. I wanted to cry just from the joy of it all. My heart was touched by a rose. Whenever I would move, she would move with me. As I walked past the other roses, they turned the same color of the rose that kissed me. So wonderful, so heartfelt! I reached out to touch the roses. They turned and reached out and touched me! I could hear soft music coming from the roses. The air smelled like so many types of fruits. The palm trees were dancing, swaying back and forth to the music.

Amazing! My vision was normal at one moment; then I could see everything in 3-D! The next moment I thought, should I say something or just enjoy the experience. I'm really enjoying this moment, so I'll keep it to myself.

I looked back at the roses, and they were clapping! I could see the palace starting to shimmer in color. It felt like the palace was alive and communicating with us, telling us to come closer. I was doing all of the talking. Keisha really didn't say too much. I guess she was letting me know she'll be here, but because I was their guest, I had to ask the questions and observe all I could so that when I returned to Earth, I could tell the story as I saw it.

The Kingdom

The kingdom was the size of several football stadiums. It didn't seem that huge coming up on it. Clouds covered half of the kingdom. That's why it didn't look so large at first. I really couldn't fathom me standing there, but we were!

As we stood outside the palace, the shimmering settled down. The clouds drifted away behind the palm trees. I took a deep breath. From what we saw, I couldn't believe how the kingdom was built. "Woosh! Woosh!" I heard! I looked to my right and my left. Both angels' wings emerged from their clothing. Fourteen feet of wings from both angels spread across the kingdom. The front door of the kingdom went from white to pure gold. This was a different type of gold. It was a beautiful gold.

Now, let me tell you the kingdom is pure white all over. From the ground, up to five feet are roses who greet you with love. Two feet up from the roses are diamonds! Yes, diamonds! Diamonds! All shapes and sizes are here. I want to say that they're made into the side of the palace, as if someone placed them one by one and side by side. I was just speechless at the wonder of it all.

Every diamond in the world is placed on the kingdom walls, from seven to hundreds of feet high. I touched them just to make sure I wasn't dreaming. From hundreds of feet to the top of the roof are crystal windows.

There isn't a word to describe what I saw. The kingdom is so gorgeous I always told my little sister how I thought the kingdom would look. I only went by what I read in the Bible and pastors have told me. I never would have believed what I had just seen, not at all. The roses are incredible. The front door was spectacular the way it changed from brick to pure gold. All the diamonds in the world were placed on the bricks of the kingdom.

With my spirit eyes I could see the top of the roof, all around the palace while standing in front of the kingdom. My eyes could turn corners. The kingdom is the size of seven stadiums. From God's purple clouds at the top of the kingdom looked like a giant cross with a diamond shaped covering that sparkled with radiant colors. It made all types of rainbows in heaven. When the sunlight shone through the top, the world's prettiest blue bounced off the walls inside, causing the whole interior to shine this calming blue. The angels commented, "Blue love is the color, Quest." I felt the love too! At the top of the kingdom stood angels with harps, horns and violins.

Butterflies and doves were flying around us and over the rooftop. Beautiful music was flowing throughout the kingdom. The doves and butterflies transformed into angels with horns and harps. They were on the top of the Kingdom playing music for us. The angels who were with us still had their wings opened. The front doors to the palace went from blending in with the sides to gold. I asked, "How?" The angels answered my question before I finished asking it. "How did you know what I was going to ask you?"

They responded, "We can read your thoughts, Quest."

"All the time?" I wanted to know.

"Yes, Quest," they said in harmony.

"How about Keisha? Can she?"

My lil' sister answered, "I can too."

"Really?" I asked. "I'm pretty impressed! So, why did the front door change from white brick to gold?"

"We're about to go in, Quest. You must have heavenly wings in order to enter God's glory light."

"How will I remember all of this? This is too much to handle. No one's going to believe me. Tell me I'm dreaming this, so I can wake up. I can't fathom what I just saw," I lamented.

"What you just saw and touched, Quest, is God's kingdom. We are here with you. You will remember what you experienced when the time comes, Quest. We believe in you, Quest. The vision is with you always. You must tell people on Earth how heaven looks. If you ever need our help, call us. Again, we can read your mind. You can revisit heaven just by blinking, Quest. Every blink will be a glimpse of heaven at any time of the day or night, Quest," they advised.

Inside the Palace

As we entered, I felt like I knew so much more than I did before. Like I became more intelligent. I kept thinking, *wow!* As I looked around, we took ten steps into the kingdom and stopped. All the angels in the palace looked straight at us. "Are they going to greet us?" I asked. Soft music was in the air, almost the perfect jazz I've ever heard. Angels were everywhere. Love was in the air. Every angel I glanced at, I felt love.

They came toward us with a warm smile, just like my lil' sister's smile. I always told her she had the warmest smile. I turned and looked at her and said, "I don't want to leave!"

"I don't want to leave you, either!" Keisha told me. "There's so much to learn up here in heaven." My spirit and my heart were pumped with love.

I could hear the other angels talking about me. "That's K. Yvonne's Big Brother, Quest. He's the special one."

"Who's his angel?" the others asked. "He hasn't requested one of us yet."

You would have thought that I was royalty. I was loving it! I felt so loved. My lil' sister had a great big smile on her face the whole time. "They really love you, Big Brother," she said.

I felt like the biggest entertainer in their world. To see all the angels were just mind-blowing. Their faces again were like transgender. I really didn't know who was male or female. Some of the angels were the same height. To see their faces in front of me was mind-boggling. We could smell the sugar cookies throughout the Kingdom. We saw stars and the sparks turned into these brilliant sparkles. Then the angels looked like mannequins, painted platinum silver. Keisha and I could see our face reflecting off of their faces. I was breathless because there were so many angels just waiting to be called upon by people on earth.

In Love with an Angel

These angels were very special angels. Their wings were larger and much more beautiful. "Whoosh!" A little baby angel just flew over my head, being chased by another little angel. Some angels had on all white, others had on red, while others had on blue or yellow. A lady angel had on the most brilliant yellow and silver. All the colors were mixed with silver, but this silver was like platinum, almost transparent, shimmering like their clothing was alive.

The angel made eye contact with me. She was on the third floor of the kingdom. Again, spirit eyes can see from a very long distance. I took one blink and she was right in front of me! Stunning! Beautiful! I couldn't stop staring at her. Her hair was long, and black, blowing with the breeze, but there wasn't a breeze blowing. Her face was beautiful. Her eyes were this deep brown, deer-shaped eyes with long eyelashes. I didn't know if she was black/white/Latina/Asian; I just didn't know. I didn't care! I felt loved. I felt the love coming from her.

"Love is colorless."

I was in love with an angel. I didn't want her to leave my side. Now my lil' sis and I already had angel escorts, but I wanted her all to myself. The other angels weren't upset at all. They knew she was there for me. What I didn't know at the time was that I had been thinking all along that I wanted an angel to be by my side, but I didn't say it out loud. I was thinking about requesting an angel and she heard my thoughts and responded to my need. Once we made eye contact I knew she was the one for me. I just looked at my lil' sis and said, "How did she move so fast? I only took a blink and she was right in front of me?"

My lil' sister said, "How amazing is that, Big Brotha?"

"I'm amazed, lil' sis. I feel like a little kid at Christmas with all these gifts to myself!"

The other angels knew her, and I was connected with the most loving grin on her face. She said, "Hello, Quest!"

"How do you know my name?" I asked. As the angel answered, my little sister began laughing.

"We all know who you are, but when you get to earth, you have to do something for me. I won't tell you now, but you'll know when the time is right and then your soul will be so much happier, but for now your spirit is good. By the way, to answer your question, my name is SrLove (Sure Love), and I love you too, Quest."

I looked at my lil' sister, and she introduced herself. As they greeted each other, I couldn't help but hold her hand. She could read what I was thinking. I'm still amazed at her name.

We held hands while "flolking" in the Kingdom. My lil' sister and I noticed there were no mirrors in the palace. Nowhere! I asked, "Why is that?"

Everyone in the kingdom is well dressed every day Sure Love answered my question, "Imagine on earth if there were no mirrors? People wouldn't act the same way. Looks wouldn't matter. You would love a person deep within first. It shouldn't matter how someone looks for a person to love them. It should be felt from your heart."

We "flolked" around God's mansion and came upon my lil' sister's room. It was huge, like an apartment! Her bed was made of clouds. A pillow was made of clouds with a silky sheet and pillowcase. It very well looked that way.

Our family pictures were taken in November. That picture sat on her dresser. Her kids and the child she lost years ago were sitting on her chest of drawers. I had never seen the child before because my lil' sis lost her around her third month. Now that I'm thinking back, the baby angel that flew past us, when we were standing at the front door was the same baby angel here with us. My lil' sis had a stillborn. I noticed that a high school picture of her, too, sat posted by her bed. Her room was a soft pink with windows that overlooked the dancing palm trees. Wow!

"Keisha, how wonderful is this?"

I noticed that there wasn't a television. At this time I heard the chimes! Clapping! Harps! Horns blowing!

"If I hear chimes, does that mean someone passed over?" I asked.

"Yes," she answered. "They have passed over and their spirit has traveled, and they have finally made it here to heaven." My hands were just kissed by my angel.

I knew my time in heaven was coming to an end. I also could see myself back on earth crying. Normally my spirit would have been blocked because of my high level of belief. I wasn't affected at all. As I put my hand straight out like a stop motion, I felt myself settling down from my tears, just like the angels taught me in the beginning when I was crying before.

My instincts became more alive, as Ty and my lil' sister and the angels were training me, preparing me for battle with any unwanted souls. I had power! Spiritual power! Nothing anyone could do to me on earth would not make me love them. Unconditional love! My spirit had changed. I've always been a loving person, but now I really want to love everyone. I was trained by angels from God's glory light.

I saw heaven as being my house, my house in spirit. I've always felt like I could read people's thoughts as a kid. Looking into their eyes, finding their spirit. Sometimes I could see a mist of smoke hovering over people. Now, I know it wasn't just a mist of smoke, but an angel hovering who just wanted to help that person, but was never asked to. If you request an angel, they will come, but it is you who must believe spiritually. They are here to help us, enlighten us, communicate with us through our five divine senses: Vision, Smell, Hearing, Feelings and Thoughts. Take all the negative thoughts and turn them into positive ideas. I could feel people's energy and sadness. I could not explain why I felt this way.

At times I could see spirits and talk with them. I could see this glowing realm around someone. I'm now trained to know what to look for when helping people. I don't go around looking for people. God places them in front of me. I get a feeling that we have met before, and it's up to me to tell that person what I've seen or what's going to happen to them.

I do like seeing angels now, but before I didn't! I was in denial. I can tell you whether you have an angel around you or not. I meet people to show them love; to heal their souls with love; to see the beauty in them. If I could touch everyone in the world with love, joy and happiness in their hearts, I would do it right now. My hands touched God's hands. My hands touched the diamonds on the palace. My hands were kissed by an angel in heaven. I've touched God's Holy Water Fountain. His hands. "I believe you can make a change. Look in the mirror and love yourself first," God told me.

My instincts were tingling. Protection is all I thought about! I must protect my lil' sister! As we and the angel escorts "flolked" from my lil' sister's room, I could hear a very frightening growl. I stood in front of Keisha to protect her. This growl sent deep chills through my body. My lil' sister wasn't even afraid! All her fears were gone. I began to feel calmer as well. No fear! Just believe, no fear! That's all I was thinking about.

The growl became intense. Growl! Growl! Looking straight ahead, the growl was coming from. No way! Keisha! No way! Again, I stood in front of my lil' sister! "I'm okay, Big Brother. Thanks!" she said.

A white tiger appeared. He didn't look that happy. "Why is he growling so loud?" I asked.

The angels explained, "Loud? He's not loud! You're scared on earth, so you're hearing this at a high level. Calm yourself down on earth and the tiger will calm down." As I calmed myself down, the tiger was calming down. told the tiger to come without moving her lips. The tiger and I connected eye-to-eye. The tiger started running toward us, growling, but not that loud. The tiger was about a hundred feet from us. He was HUGE! Then he jumped in the air toward us!

I wondered why he jumped from so far away, a hundred foot leap! At that moment my vision was the same way as if I were back at my house, looking at that bird. I could zoom in and out, top and bottom, at the same time. The tiger and I glanced eye-to-eye, as he began to approach. Because my spirit level was so high, I could see straight through the tiger. I saw all the pretty stripes. His coat was beautiful. He jumped in the air again toward us and I slowed his motion, stopping him in midair, walking under him! I could touch his teeth, hair, nose, ears, tail, paws, claws, and his chest.

As he continued in slow motion, I stood by my lil' sister and with Keisha's angels beside us. The tiger landed and walked toward us. His head was very HUGE. His body was ten feet long! I stepped forward, but he didn't want me to come near him. I felt a connection with this tiger. He bypassed me and walked right up to Keisha. My lil' sister bent down toward the tiger's face. I was thinking how he could have bitten her whole face off, but he wasn't just any tiger. My lil' sister whispered to her angels, "I've seen those eyes before."

"Yes, K. Yvonne, you have. You've seen those eyes your whole life," the angels responded.

"I don't understand," she said, looking so confused.

I noticed the tiger had a mole on his cheek bone, under his right eye. "How pretty is that?" I asked.

She said, "I get to look at you everyday."

"Me?" I asked my lil' sister's angels, but before I could finish getting my sentence out, they answered me, too!

"Yes, you, Quest." I looked at Keisha because I was really confused then. At that time I heard rumbling in the air. As we looked up, there were clouds in the palace. Breath-taking, purple clouds that sparkled.

Keisha said, "Oooooh! Now I know where I saw this Tiger before: your house, Big Brother! On your wall!" "Oh, that's right, Keisha! Girl, now you're thinking!" I said.

"Not only the picture on the wall, but if you look really close at the tiger, his face looks like your brother's, face. If your brother were an animal, he would be a tiger. That's why the tiger bypassed him earlier, as if he were looking at himself." Explained Keisha's angels.

"Hello, my son!" I heard this very deep voice greeting me.

"Is that the clouds?"

"Yes, Quest, it's God." My mind went blank! I looked at my lil' sister and God spoke again, "Hello my child. Welcome home." I stood there shaking my head back and forth. "Wow! Wow!"

God spoke to me, "My son, Quest. K. Yvonne brought you to the kingdom so that you could see and touch things. It is I who gave you the gift of light for you to tell others what you've experienced here in heaven. What I have shown you, others will be envious and jealous of you, my son. Keep your faith! Believe in yourself, always. I've shown you my kingdom and how you, my son, can tell people whom I bring into your life. Share the glory experience to others who need your help. You are special, my son, Quest."

"I will, God. I will help people you bring in front of me or into my life."

God Spoke to My Lil' Sister

"My child, Keisha. You must care for this tiger, Keisha. This is your animal. I love you, my child." Keisha and I looked at each other in amazement!

Keisha's angels told her, "Keisha, that tiger is not just any tiger. He is in your brother's likeness, Keisha."

I could feel my vision getting blurry. Earth Quest was crying, blocking one-third of my spiritual connection.

Keisha began to question, "My Brother? Why my big brother?" They asked, "You wouldn't hurt your brother, would you, K.Yvonne?"

"No! Never!" she replied.

I kissed her on the cheek and said, "I love you for coming to me to calm my spirit down and for showing me heaven. I've learned so much. I don't really want to go back. I'm going to miss my sister so much! How long have we been up here in heaven?"

All the angels turned their heads toward us and said in harmony, "All day!" I could see the clock in my house from heaven. The time was 8:21. That's one hour on earth, but it didn't seem like it.

They said, "You are a quick learner. There will be more to learn on earth, Quest. Your lil' sister can show you and teach you other things so you will know, and if she doesn't know, you can always ask S'rlove, your angel."

I could feel myself really crying on earth. My spirit connection was coming down. I didn't want to let S'rlove's hand go. I didn't want to leave all these lovely angels.

My lil' sister inquired, "So, I get to see Marvin Gaye? I get to be with a white tiger that nobody has? I get to fly in paradise whenever

I want to?" At that moment I felt like crying in heaven. No one cries in heaven because there's nothing but joy. My eyes started blinking because I was crying for so long on earth.

Keisha consoled me, "It's okay, Big Brother. I'm okay now. I have you by my side. Plus, S'rlove is here with me. She is so pretty. Boy! You're so lucky."

I'm okay with myself crying on earth. I could feel my spirit draining, coming back to earth. I hugged my lil' sister and her angels and kissed their cheeks. I could feel their love, not wanting me to leave.

As I "flolked" from the palace, my beauty rose gave me a kiss on my cheek. I could feel her love wanting me to stay as well.

My lil' sister and her angels stood back while I "flolked" toward those brilliant orange clouds. A rainbow drifted over the palace, as if the palace was saying good-bye to me. My lil' sister said, looking over her shoulder with a single tear in her eye, "Big, Brother , I love you so much. I will always have you by my side, always, Big Brother. I don't want to tell you good-bye, but on earth, I'm not there anymore. As much as this pains me, you must say good-bye to me for now. I am at peace and there's no more pain. You must understand and love me in your spirit. Tell Mom and Dad that I love them with all my heart. I had the strength from mom and the artistic senses from dad! What a wonderful combination! Without you all, there is no me! And I wouldn't be here in heaven. I'm okay! May your lives continue to be filled with blessings, and I love you."

My mind went blank. I could feel my heart slow down. Losing a loved one or someone dear to you really makes you think about life, their good memories and laughter. Just standing there in heaven with my lil' sister was a blessing from God, but again, my mind went blank!

I didn't want to leave my lil' sister. "Wait! Please tell me more. Can I stay just a couple of minutes more? Please, Keisha, don't go! I love you so much! Wait! I love you so much! You need me! I need you! Wait! Don't go! I love you so much! Please God! Please God, tell me this is a dream! Please!"

As my earth spirit cried heavily, it made my heaven spirit level go down, making me drift away from my lil' sister. Keisha was flolking toward the front doors, walking with the tiger, rubbing his head, both angels trailing behind her.

"Wait, don't go!" I begged. My lil' sister, looking back over her shoulder, calling to me, "Big Brotha, I'm gonna be up here for a while. Tell the family and my friends, Mom, Dad, Ty, Apria, O'shea, Cierra, Sabian and J'waun Tyrone I love them and I love Ty and you, Big Brother!"

"Don't go! S'rlove, help me. "Don't Go, Keisha! I love you so much. What am I to do without you? Please God! S'rlove, S'rlove, God!" I cried as I drifted back to earth, falling through the clouds.

As her face appeared in the clouds, Keshia called to me, "Big Brother! I love you too! I guess I'll see you in heaven!"

"Keisha! Don't do this to me," I cried. As I fell out of the sky with my arms limp, I could feel the air on my back. My head and my body were motionless. I had my eyes closed because I just didn't care at that moment. Everything I've learned in heaven was racing through my mind so fast. The memories of my lil' sister made my heart even sadder. I could feel myself crying so loud! No one could hear me because I was falling from heaven. "Please, God, let me bring my sister back with me. Please don't do this to me. I love her so much," I prayed. My last thought was my little sister running toward me with her arms outstretched with this big smile on her face, so happy to see me!

I could see my house with my spiritual vision, but I didn't want to come back. As I was falling, I could feel my spiritual instincts kick in.

Pages of Tears

I heard, "Big Brother, open your eyes." Again, I heard, "Quest, open your eyes." As my eyes slowly opened, my lil' sister and S'rlove were together calling, "Quest!" They appeared with a mist of sparkling colors of purple, yellow, silver and brilliant orange clouds. Then I saw a burst of beautiful stars. My lil' sister appeared to have larger wings. She wasn't wearing this in heaven. I recalled her wings when spread out were silver in color.

My lil' sister and S'rlove came flying out of the clouds to rescue me as I was falling. I closed my eyes with my arms and body motionless. I passed out for a second. I could hear their voices calling my name over and over, "Quest, wake up! Quest, wake up! Believe, Quest! We are here to rescue you!" I woke up and could see them coming faster and faster. "We got you, Quest! We won't let you fall, going back to earth, Quest."

"I love you and my lil' sister so much. Why should I return home? Why?" I asked.

"We will always be here for you. always, Quest." I didn't know I was already home, standing in my living room. They could see the earth Quest crying at the table. S'rlove placed her hand on my shoulders. She leaned down and said, "Quest, you will be okay. I love you. Your lil' sister loves you. Relax. Breathe. We love you, Quest."

I said, "I love you so much, and you too, Keisha. I love you so much!"

"I love you too, Big Brother," she said.

I Believe

I held my head down. When I looked up, my heavenly spirit walked toward me, then stepped into my body. I felt very happy and full of love. I stopped crying, now full of love.

When I returned to my body, I knew I felt different, but at first I thought that maybe I had fallen asleep and dreamed all of this.

Then God spoke, "My son, Quest! Don't worry what people think of you. So many people, family and friends are going to envy you, my son, for what I have shown you. They will believe you. I will place people in your life for you to share this heavenly experience with, Quest. They will believe you. If they don't believe you, they will come back to you one day. Be ready, my son, Quest. Look them in their eyes and connect with their spirit. It is you, my son, Quest, I have chosen to share my glory light. It is you, my son, Quest that believes and has faith. You will not remember everything I have shown you. Only certain parts of this experience will remain fresh in your mind. When you start to write this experience, to share with the world, it is only then you will remember everything I have shown you, my son, Quest. With every blink you will see heaven like you've never seen it before but this time more intense. Your handwriting will change, for it is not only you writing this experience by yourself; you're writing this experience with your angel. Do not question yourself. Write it as you see it. It will come to you as fast as you receive it. Take care, my son, Quest. "God, I do believe," I told myself over and over again!

At the Table

Why is my shirt so wet? I'm warm and sweating, I'm wondering to myself as I sat at the table and my mind was so far gone. I must be hallucinating! I looked at the time. I even checked the date. I didn't know what to do. I took a shower and got dressed. I woke my son and nephew. I couldn't believe they were asleep this whole time!

I could hear my lil' sister's voice, so faintly, "I told you I had that under control, Big Brother!"

"So, I wasn't hallucinating," I said to her.

"No," she said. "So, why can I still hear you?"

"Because I'm here with you," Keisha answered. "I've come back to train you."

"Train me? On what? I thought I was finished?"

"No, Big Brother, I have to teach you about numbers and what they mean. Also, about clouds and stars." "Really? How long is that going to take," I wanted to know.

"Hm, seven days," she responded.

"Why seven days? I'm still kind of lost about the whole heaven experience. Why do I feel like I know so much, but I can't explain it?" I inquired.

"It'll all come back to you when you start writing the book."

"What book?" I asked a little bewildered.

"The book! Your day in heaven," she replied.

"I'm going to write a book?" I questioned. "Yeah, right! People are going to think I'm crazy or I'm hallucinating. The whole story?"

"Story? This is real, Big Brother. Who do you think you're talking to?" asked my lil' sister. A part of me didn't want to look behind me to see if this experience was real. As I stood in my hallway, I could hear my little sister's voice behind me saying, "If you're listening to me, then you believe that you're talking to me. Why not believe that I'm behind you?" she said even before I could turn around. As I turned around, the hallway had so many little stars, like white Christmas lights on a tree. Her body was glowing. I could see her face.

Teach Me

Keisha explained that over the next seven days she would teach me about clouds, numbers, and how I could communicate with the angels. S'rlove would teach me how to hear music in the air and to use my spiritual connection at a higher level and about looking at angels.

I walked out from my room thinking my son and nephew probably heard everything, but they didn't because they were sound asleep. I really wish they could have heard or seen what I went through. This heaven experience would be much easier to explain to them if they had. The fact that I didn't say anything to them, and I kept it to myself didn't make it any easier to be able to explain to people about my magical experience.

My lil' sister was gone, so I went back to my room, still in disbelief. My thoughts were: six days of training; the whole angel experience; God; palace; flying through clouds, the ocean water; the dolphins. As I sat there, I couldn't remember much more than that. I was very happy to have experienced heaven, but now what? I had to tell my family, but how? I heard my lil' sister's voice saying, "I'll be with you, Big Brother, when you tell them, okay?"

"Why do you think Ma and Dad are going to believe me, Keisha?" I asked.

"Trust me, they will!" she answered.

Mom, Have a Seat

On February 21, 2009, after I went to heaven and came back, I knew I had to tell my mother. God told me so. He said, "My son, Quest, have your mother sit down and take a deep breath. Your heaven experience will touch her heart and others. This will bring relief to her mother grief and will make her soul and heart feel so beautiful. Look your mother directly in her eyes when you tell her about this event. Have a good day, my son, Quest."

I picked up my keys and jumped into my truck. As I started driving to my parents' house, I was so excited. I went up to the house, and all my brothers and sisters were there. My dad came in the house just as I had entered.

After I explained my experience to the family, my mother looked at me and said, "I knew you were special, some kind of medium. I knew it! That explains to me all those other times too, that you had angels with you all those years ago. Now this all makes sense to me. You and Keisha were mediums or angels. Keisha could foresee what was going to happen to people."

I said, "Ma, I've been in denial for years about my gift. I thought I was crazy as a kid. I could feel people around me, sometimes seeing them in my dreams, but they weren't dreams. I know that now."

I hugged my mother and said, "I love you, Ma! Keisha is okay now."

As I told my heavenly experience to my family, they all had the same look on their faces – eyes wide opened and mouth slightly opened like they were saying, "Aaaaah!" This was my "coming out experience" to my whole family. My parents had known I was different as a child. I knew I was, too. I was just in denial for years. As I told my experience, Keisha was there in the house looking right at me. She was standing by my mother first, then my dad. I stopped talking because I thought they could see her. My event was short for what I could only remember. The family was amazed and asked a whole lot of questions. They had so many questions to ask me! I really felt this experience brought each of us closer as a family. Our love was stronger than ever. My "Seven Days" of learning had begun.

As I had driven over to my parents' house, I noticed the same cloud had followed me. I kept seeing the same numbers pass by me, 7/23/218. When I went to the store on my way there, the total of my purchases was $2.18. I put gas in my truck at Pump #7. When I parked my truck in front of my parent's house, I took twenty-three steps from my truck to the front door.

Clouds

On February 22, 2009, my lil' sister came to me spiritually. She told me all about clouds, what they really are saying to us. I never knew about clouds, only what I'd learned in school. Angels are in clouds, showing us something every day. We just don't pay them any attention at all. Before now, I didn't either. From what I know now, I look in the sky every day. My lil' sister explained, "When your spiritual realm is at a high level and you hear music, always look to the clouds. Your loved ones will create a special cloud for us. Sometimes that cloud looks just like the person's face." I look at clouds on clear, sunny days, around 10:30 or 11:00 and I look around the sun.

Have you ever seen a "rainbow cloud?" They're beautiful! Thanks to my lil' sister, I see them all the time. When I hear music in the air, I know there are angel clouds in the sky. You'll know when you see angel clouds. They look like angels! I hope you love looking at the clouds like I do.

Before Keisha died, I could hear music in the air. I just couldn't explain it. I heard chimes and horns the most. Everything else I heard, I can't explain the type of instruments that I heard. Every time I hear chimes, I think about my lil' sister. It was told to me that only people with a high spiritual connection could hear angels talking to them. Sometimes I wake up to chimes playing in the air. It's so relaxing and beautiful to hear. Now that my spiritual realm is at a high level, the music I hear in the air is so clear. It's the perfect jazz concert.

What Do Numbers Mean?

Angels communicate with you through numbers. When your loved one passes away, look at the time; their house address; license plate number; their age; when you go to the store, the total of your purchase, and the change from the purchase. You will be surprised how all the numbers come out the same. When my lil' sister passed away, the numbers 7*2*3* and 2*1*8 kept coming up. My lil' sister's birthday is March 14 (7x2=14/3). I bought a newspaper and some gum. The total with taxes was $2.18 (2*1*8). My lil' sister's apartment door was the seventh door. From the front door to her door was twenty-three steps (7*2*3). My lil' sister's resting place is 23 steps from the side of "The Cross" which is the number "7." I was so into numbers after my lil' sister passed away because I wanted to know more. There is a book entitled *Angel Numbers 101* by Doreen Virtue that I had to get, so I could see what the angels and my lil' sister were telling me. You will not be the same once you start communicating with angels or your loved one. They will tell you special messages, so please, listen and pay attention to them.

The Last Walk

On February 25, 2009, my lil' sister was buried at the cemetery. As I rode to the church, I stopped to get gas. All the pumps were taken, but one. Pump #4 was open. I went inside to pay the attendant a twenty dollar bill. I could hear my lil' sister's voice, faintly saying, "fourteen dollars, Big Brother." I looked around thinking people could hear her, but they couldn't. "Uh, 14 on Pump 14," I instructed the attendant. I knew my lil' sister was trying to tell me something. She was "29" when she died. I brought the book *Angel Numbers 101*, by Doreen Virtue to help me with angel numbers. This book has really helped me learn so much about numbers. Driving to the church, I could smell my lil' sister, so I knew she was riding in the truck with me. Nothing was said to me, so I knew she was just passing by and doing the same thing with other family members. Walking to the front doors of the church, I was calm, until I opened the doors and could feel my lil' sister all over me. I could hear her voice very clear, "It's going to be okay, Big Brother. Believe! You can do this! You have to do this today for me!

Lost without My Lil' Sister

Sitting there in the pew with my other family members, I remember zoning out when other family members passed me, asking if I was okay. All I heard was "Yeah, we're here if you need us, okay?" But, when my mother, father or Ty came near, I lost it! I started crying uncontrollably. I knew our family wouldn't be the same after this day. I felt my heart taken from me and I couldn't find it. No one could find my heart, no one! "Lost! I Lost my Heart!"

When you love someone with your heart, it's pure love. I loved what Keisha and I had. It was special. A little sister is a good friend for life. And I just lost a good friend for life! Lost!

I would let her win when we would race, just so I could hear her laugh! I remember bringing her a lollipop because she was putting her makeup on for the first time, looking like a clown, but she didn't know that. She just trusted me. When I used to go pick her up from daycare, she would come running out of the school, arms outstretched smiling from ear to ear. "Big Brother," she would call, "Big Brother!" Just like she hadn't seen me all year. "I have so much to show you what I made for you today, Big Brother!"

Pages of Tears

As I prepared myself to view my lil' sister's body, I could hear her quietly talking to me. My spirit level was lower than usual because I had started to cry. My uncle Jake was my escort. He understood my grief because he had lost his son, Spike, ten years ago to gun violence. I love him for being there with me. I'm not a small person. My uncle is shorter and smaller. As I approached her casket, my crying intensified, my body became numb, and my legs turned into rubber. My head bent backwards like I was going to faint. My lil' sister's voice said, "Oh, no you're Not, Big Brother! I need you to be strong so others can draw their strength from you."

I approached the casket. My uncle Jake encouraged me, "Come on, man, be strong!"

I cried, "I can't bear to see her like this."

My lil' sister asked, "What do you mean? You have to see me Big Brother! I'm your lil' sister. Uncle Jake," I heard her say. I could feel my heartbeat slowing down. I knew I wasn't going to make it.

"I'm not going to make it. I'm so sorry, Keisha. I'm not going to make it. My heart is in too much pain," I lamented. I really began to feel my heartbeat coming to a light pulse. I could see Uncle Jake's son, Spike, helping him hold me up. I knew that I wasn't going to make it. I was dying right in front of my lil' sister. My vision became hazy. All I saw was white.

I could hear my heart slowing down. Bump, bump, bump. My uncle Jake said, "Hey man! Have a seat." I heard my heartbeat. I wasn't normal, I needed help. My uncle didn't know that, but I knew.

My vision became blurrier, but I could still hear. My uncle Jake didn't know what state I was in. My eyes slightly closed, I was looking at the slide show of my lil' sister. As I sat there dying, Keisha said, "Hey, Big Brother! Remember these pictures? Just like in heaven."

"It's too much to handle, Keisha I'm sorry. I'm sorry. I love you, Mom, Dad, Ty, I'm sorry," is all I could say.

As I sat there motionless, no one knew anything. I heard my uncle's voice, "Take a rest, son." My lil' sister started shouting, "Please! Someone help my brother! Not my brother! Not today!"

Angels stood by her casket, some flying around the room. Several angels were present, big and small. "Please help my big brother!"

One angel answered, "We will! Is your big brother saved?"

"I don't know," responded my lil' sister. We used to always go to church. Save him!"

"If your Big Brother were saved, he could see and hear so much more in the spirit world," the angels told her.

"He'll be saved today. He will. He was as a teenager, but drifted away from church when he got older. Please help him," she begged them.

Her angel said, "He can hear us. He can request his helping angel to save him. At a blink of an eye, he'll be here." "Quest, request a helping angel," my lil' sister said. "Big Brother! Can you hear me? Ask for an angel!" she yelled.

Ask for an Angel

"I can hear you, Keisha! I need a helping angel. Please come help me!" I screamed! I could smell this angel coming. I heard him with a strong voice, "Sit up, QUEST! Take a deep breath. God has sent me to help you. You requested help." I stood up, crying.

Whoosh! This angel came down in front of me from the ceiling. He stood right there in front of me, "flolking" toward me. "I'm here for you, Quest. Take a deep breath. Your heart is not well. There's only one thing I can do."

"What's that," I asked.

He turned around. The smell of sugar cookies filled the air. I asked him, "What's next?" He took a step backwards, his hair touching my nose, then walked through me. He put his wings straight out. I felt energized to the max, like being shocked, but this was all love. "Take a deep breath, Quest." My breathing became more normal, and my heartbeat was normal. As I walked toward my lil' sister's casket, I kept touching my face, left side, right side. His feathers were touching my face. He put his wings straight out, all sixteen feet, straight out.

Angel Bariel

No one walked past me. I still couldn't look at my lil' sister in that lovely casket she was laying in. I walked past it, taking the first chair I saw, my uncle by my side.

Angel Bariel spoke, "Quest, take fourteen deep breaths for me. With every breath, you will have a good memory of your lil' sister. I complied and began to feel stronger with every breath I took. My vision was in tact. I could see clearly again. "Stand up by yourself, Quest."

My uncle looked and spoke, "You sure you can handle this by yourself, son?"

"Yes, I feel good," I said with a smile. I got up and could feel everyone looking at me. I could hear their thoughts. I knew that I was okay, walking to the open casket, smiling as I went along. I could feel my lil' sister giving me hugs and kisses just like when she was five years old again. I started laughing and smiling, holding her hand.

Angel Bariel stood in back of me, with his wings spread apart. No one walked up at all. This was my healing time. I said, "Thank you, Keisha, for what you've done for me. I've lost you on earth, but I can be with you every day in the spiritual world."

My lil' sister was still hugging me, not wanting to let me go.

My lil' sister, "I know Big Brother. I had to come back and get you."

As I left her casket, I turned and gave my mother, a hug for her Keisha and myself.

"I'm okay, Ma! She's okay too I love you, Ma!" I sat in my chair and heard all this cheering, music and clapping.

Angel Bariel explained, "Quest, you're okay now, my job is done here."

"Thank you," I said.

"We're so happy and joyful for you, Quest. K.Yvonne is very happy for you too!" said the angels. "You're welcome, Quest." Then they all flew away.

I heard a soft voice with beautiful celestial music playing, "Hello, Quest." I became really joyful and happy knowing who that was. S'rlove! "We heard you're going to get saved today."

"Yes, I am so I can continue to make my spiritual connection stronger."

"This is one of the things I was talking about you doing once you get back to earth," S'rlove said.

Our Last Tear Together

I walked back over to view the casket a couple more times. I couldn't bear to even look at her. I remembered my legs feeling like rubber. I heard later that my helping angel, Bariel, was carrying me to and from the casket. All I kept doing was wiping my face, left and right from his feathers. He had one wing spread straight out and the other around me, like he was giving me time to heal. When I started to calm down and relax, Angel Bariel left my side. He looked over his shoulder and said, "You're okay now, Quest. If you need me, call me. We're always here to help you, Quest."

As my lil' sister lay there in this beautiful white and gold casket, I knew my time was limited from seeing her once more. I could hear the soft music in the background getting louder. It was time to close the casket. To see my beautiful lil sister lying there motionless, knowing this is "it." I could feel my lil' sis touching me. With her right hand, she placed it over my heart. Her left hand softly wiped my tears away. She said, "I'm okay now, Big Brother. You don't have to cry for me anymore. Hey, we went to heaven together, just like we said we were going to do. Remember?" With tears streaming down my face, hiding behind my sunglasses, I got up one last time before the casket closed. I leaned down with tears and kissed Keisha on her cheek. I noticed my tears touched her face. As they rolled down her face, it looked like her last loving tear that never fell.

Angels Communicating

Minister Stanton asked if anyone wanted to be saved and have Jesus come into their hearts and forgive them of all their sins. I sat waiting. I told myself I was already saved. But I wasn't. Again, I heard cheering from angels waiting for more "names in their book." That's when I saw a small angel with wings, flying and hovering over my brother and I. I saw my brother jump as if someone tried to pick him up. I could feel my suit jacket lift up. I got up and walked over to Minister Stanton, looking eye-to-eye. I could feel his spirit. "Good," he said. Here came my brother. My son, my sister's kids, my cousin that I haven't seen in twenty years, and my lil' sister's daughter's father. We all stood holding hands, embracing one another. We asked for forgiveness, prayed and put our name in the Angel Book. I stood there loving this man, heart-to-heart. Thank you so much and I love you for guiding me, helping me to start a new life, Minister Billy Stanton, Jr.

Leaving the church, my mind was thinking about "723." I don't know why I was thinking of those numbers. As we entered the resurrection, I started hearing voices. "Please help me. Can you help me, too?"

"No, he can't! That's my big brother! He's here for me only. Tell them you're here for your lil' sister only, Big Brother," she said. As I explained to them that I was here for my lil' sister, the voices drifted away.

I sat there starting to cry. I had cried so much I was all cried out of tears. I took a flower off her casket, just held it as if she had given it to me.

"723" stuck in my head. "I need help with this one, Keisha, I'm stuck," I said.

My lil' sister said, "I can't think about numbers now." Prayer ended and we all went back to the church to meet and greet. I sat by my mother at the table, feeling really happy and joyful. I wanted to thank everyone for coming to show my lil' sister love.

I love you all. Thank you so much.

As we left the church and went back to my parents' house, I wanted to tell everyone who asked me about my experience in heaven, but I didn't. I stayed to myself and sat by my mother all evening. My lil' sister was there standing beside my mother all the time. Why no one could see this hazy mist behind my mother amazed me. So, I took a picture of my mother sitting there with her shadow missing. The sunlight beamed through the curtains, making my mother's shadow appear, but because my lil' sister was standing behind her, there was no shadow. As the day was coming to an end, I knew I should share this event with others, but not now. In the meantime, I've experienced other special events that amazed me.

When my lil' sister passed away, the numbers "723" kept coming up. I would go to the store and buy something. My total came to $7.23. My mother, finished doing my lil' sister's paperwork, she looked at her watch. The time was 7:23. This number had the whole family wondering, "What was the meaning?' It stayed on my mind.

Every day!

Every night!

On March 14, 2009 at 7:47 p.m., I walked into my bathroom. I felt kind of dizzy, so I sat on the toilet. I looked down at the rugs on the floor. Wow! There were three faces of Jesus. I could hear my lil' sister's voice faintly telling me "Think."

I got dressed and took my sons with me to the cemetery. I got out of my truck. I raced to her plot, yelling, "I figured it out!" I stood over my lil' sister's grave site and spoke to her, "I know what "723" means."

"Do I take twenty three steps and look up at the clouds in the sky?" I asked.

"You're close. That's not it," she replied.

"No!" I exclaimed, shaking my head back and forth, stopping at the cross.

My lil' sister said, "Yes! You know what 723 means!"

"Wow! Wow!" My lil' sister said, "You're getting good, Big Brother."

"If I take twenty-three steps toward the cross, my last step would be at the mark of the cross. Since we hadn't gotten a tombstone yet, and if it snowed, we would always know how to find her by taking those twenty-three steps from the cross to her grave.

Seeing the three faces of Jesus in my rug gave me the chills. As I entered the cemetery, there was the first face. As I walked the grounds, I noticed the second face. It started raining, so we all ran toward the middle with all the trees.

I turned around, and Jesus's statue was right in front of me, shielding us from the lightening and rain! It stopped raining when I touched his feet.

We heard a scream.

My lil' sister asked, "You want to see something that will blow your mind, Big Brother?"

"Yeah, show me!" The scream got louder! We walked through some bushes.

"You see that?" she asked.

"Yes! A peacock!" I exclaimed. I've never seen a peacock in person before, but it was here today right in front of us. As I opened my palm, it came right to me. At every step it took toward me, I became calmer. It was like he was communicating with me.

My lil' sister instructed, "Close your hand." As I did, it stopped. "Watch this," she said.

WHOOSH! The peacock's feathers opened up in front of my eyes. I touched it softly.

When I went to heaven I saw all those angels who were waiting to be called. They would answer prayers if you would call upon them to help you. I didn't believe in angels at first. Months before my lil' sister's death, I was sleeping with the TV on. People were talking about angels.

This show was on for thirty minutes. While I slept I envisioned everything they were talking about. I turned over on the remote and the TV blinked off. The remote fell to the floor. That's when I heard the TV blink on right at the beginning. "Do You Believe in Angels? Are Angels Real?"

This time I got up to look at it. How? Who turned my TV on? An angel did!

Angels smell like sugar cookies and smoke. I could smell that in the air. I watched the show and was amazed. I started noticing things people around me didn't see. I felt so happy all the time, even when I was feeling down. I started getting depressed over things in my life that weren't going right.

I would call to talk to my lil' sister about my feelings. Come to find out, she was going through the same thing. We would start laughing. I'd crack a joke just to hear her laugh and that would make me feel so much better and loved. Always call someone you love when you're feeling down and depressed. Love makes the heart smile.

When my lil' sister passed away, I could see her on earth or in the clouds. When night time came, I would feel so depressed knowing I had to wait until the sun came up again the next morning in order to see her. I heard my lil' sisters' voice, "Nope! You don't. You can see me in the stars at night."

The first time I tried the Face in the Stars experience, I didn't know what effect it was going to have. I picked a clear night when the stars were shining brightly. I made sure that I had a good camera. I then cleared my mind, took a deep breath and then another deep breath. I thought of happy thoughts of my lil' sister and pointed the camera toward the stars. I put my finger on the button and then closed my eyes. When I opened my eyes, I clicked the flash button. I then saw my little sister's face in the stars.

When I did this the first time, I was astounded. I did it over and over again. Then I showed my mother, brothers, and sisters. They too were amazed. My angel showed me that experience.

On February 22, 2009 at 5:30 p.m. I experienced something wonderful. I was in a restaurant with my family. We sat down to eat. I heard, "Hey can I show you something?"

I said, "Yeah!" I looked over my shoulder because I thought it was my friend's daughter. As I noticed, she was eating and hadn't gotten up to ask me anything. I knew it was my lil' sister talking to me in front of my friend. "I don't want to start crying now. Please don't do this to me now, Keisha," I said.

"But I want to show you something," Keisha insisted. The sun started to beam on my back. I looked at my friend's daughter because I thought she could hear my lil' sister's voice. She couldn't, but my lil' sister was speaking in a normal tone.

I said, "Let's go. That sun is really beaming."

When I got outside, my lil' sister said, "Just look at the sun. Blink, then look back at the sun. I'm right beside the sun. Use your spiritual eye, Big Brother." I did it! I could see her. I wanted to cry. My eyes welled up with tears. "This is where I am right now, going into the Kingdom. Soon I will take a nap with the white tiger walking around me," Keisha explained.

I shouted for someone to bring me my phone, which was charging up. When I receive my phone, I took a video of the whole experience, the clouds with the kingdom sitting on top; her lying on a pillow cloud; the white tiger.

This was so magical for my family to see what I've been experiencing. I knew if they saw it before I said anything, they would feel like I felt, scared, but love from the clouds. My son, Quest, saw the tiger in the clouds while I just videotaped everything. He even saw my lil' sister lying on a pillow with the tiger walking around her. I say walking around because the tiger cloud was moving, but my lil' sister's cloud wasn't. My family shared this experience with me. I'm so joyful they felt her spirit from the clouds to the chills going through their bodies. When I looked at all their faces, they all had the same look, just as I did when looking in the mirror. Their pupils were dilated. No one was the same after that. I could tell that this experience made them very happy and joyful. I felt the same way. Every event makes me more grateful than the last.

Thank you, God!

I started taking pictures as if I were on the red carpet. I stopped at the gas station by my mother's house. Her house was the best place to take the photographs. I snapped the camera but erased it thinking the photo wouldn't come out. My lil' sister said, "Don't erase them! You're a second behind when you take a picture, so don't erase!"

On February 22, 2009, I heard my lil' sister's voice telling me to video tape the sun. She said, "Watch how the video turns out. It's going to amaze you, Big Brother." My family and I stopped at the gas station near my parents' house. "Start recording now, Big Brother," she instructed. In order for me to get a good video shot, I would have to cross the street. How was I going to do that when there were cars passing on both sides of the street. The light is green so the cars don't have to stop. "It's now, Big Brother!" Keisha said. I was looking at the green light. Suddenly it turned red just like that! "Don't ever erase your pictures or videos. You're a second behind when you take them, so don't erase, never, okay, Big Brother," she asked.

"Okay, lil' sister," I replied. I stood there taking pictures and videos. When I was finished, I jumped back in my truck to follow the sun. This was one of the most beautiful sunsets ever!

I took several more pictures, not really knowing how they would turn out. Afterwards, as my family stood there amazed. I started filming what was in front of me. I kept filming until my camera stopped. One video I took while passing a telephone pole with the sunlight in the background. It didn't look like much when I drove passed it, but when I played it back, the pole looked like the cross with God's light touching the pole. The pole looked like it was floating under God's light. Amazing!

When My Lil' Sister Died

On February 18, 2009, my lil' sister died in her room, in her house, her body blue, cold and motionless. The Emergency Medical Technicians tried to get a heartbeat. They pronounced her dead at the hospital. My lil' sister's spirit left her body because life was just too much for her bear. She saw herself lying on the bed and then on the floor. She was in the spiritual realm. When a death is traumatic, the spirit leaves the body very quickly before the death occurs. My lil' sister watched herself go through the painthough her spirit was already at peace. She waited for somebody's spiritual connection to be open to communicate with her. My spiritual realm was opened; that's why we communicated in the hospital. That's why I could hear her before she died. At her death she was given a choice: move on freely or remain here on earth until she was buried. She remained here on earth to comfort me and my family. She rode in the van with my mother several times. She even told my mother to check the van out before buying it.

Keisha even opened the door for my mother at times, made my other sister's clock stop at a specific time, danced in my kitchen and made a CD that I was playing stop and spin counter-clockwise, playing the song over and over again. She showed herself to my younger sister, Apria, causing her to burst out in tears. She even visited her son, J'waun, in school. My lil' sister was not ready to leave earth yet. She didn't know she had died yet. She told me she saw herself motionless in the hospital. When the doctors pronounced her dead, she said, "What do you mean I'm dead? I'm not dead! I can see my family! I spoke to my Big Brother! He can see and talk to me." I didn't want to believe that my lil' sister had died. We all didn't want to believe, so she didn't think she had died. "Not me! I'm still young! I haven't turned thirty yet," she cried. It's so painful to tell a loved one that they've died. To see that loved one in the spirit world is amazing. I hear my lil' sister's voice to this day, "What do you mean I died, Big Brother? Why me, Big Brother? Are you serious? I'm only twenty-eight!"

On March 17, 2009, I was baptized in the church. I wanted my soul to be cleansed. I felt good starting over and going back to church. I sat there during the ceremony thinking, *I want to be closer to my lil' sister's spirit. I want to go to heaven again, this time being baptized.* The first prayer was given by Reverend Simms. I closed my eyes. I started seeing sparkles. I opened them for a moment, just to make sure the room I was in didn't have any special trick lighting. I closed my eyes again. The sparkles came back and started going clockwise. The sparkles were silver, brilliant green, purple, yellow, orange, white, *bang*! They burst into a million stars. I could hear my lil' sister's voice, "Hey, Big Brother! How have you been?" I started to cry. She said, "Don't start crying! I'm happy for you!"

"I miss you, Keisha. I love you so much! I'm sorry for crying, I'm just happy to see you." I replied. The stars were moving, forming a picture. The stars went dim, then burst into more stars that formed into my lil' sister's face. I had my head down, hiding my tears.

"Can you look at me," she asked. My head was up, but my eyes were closed. "This is your day, Big Brother. I'm so happy for you!"

I asked her, "What's up with all those stars? It's beautiful. You look amazing, Keisha!" She smiled with the brightest stars as her teeth. "Just keep teaching and training me for what I have to learn, Keisha."

"I will and I'll see you later, Big Brother."

I opened my eyes and walked to the platform to talk to Reverend Berkley. I gave my name. I walked into the water, *whoosh*! Reverend Berkley held me and bent me down into the water. When I came up, I felt anew. Jesus died for me and my sins, and rose from the dead. I believe that! I was saved on February 25, 2009!

As the Reverend placed me under the water, I could see my lil' sister hovering over me. Stars! Stars! "Look at me" she demanded! I opened my eyes under water, looking right at her. When the Reverend brought me back up out of the water, I felt so refreshed, joyful. I wanted to tell everyone present, "I love you! Thank you all!" I wondered if they could see what I'd seen.

Questions People Ask Me

How did you feel going to heaven?

Extraordinary! To go to paradise was magnificent to see and be a part of this experience.

God allowed me to go to heaven without crossing over yet. I felt really loved. There aren't many people living who experienced heaven as I did. I enjoyed every minute of heaven. All of the angels I've seen; butterflies transforming into angels. There's no word on earth that I could use that really describes how I felt.

Some people asked me, "What did the floor look like in the palace."

"Crystal floors. I could see clouds moving under me all the time."

When you first see the floor, you know you're not on earth. If your house was made from the best crystal, would you build it? I would! In the spirit world, you're not worrying about your neighbors or anyone destroying your house. You can see through so many objects, it's amazing. If the Statue of Liberty was made of crystal, people would be afraid to climb the stairs because they could see through it. There's no fear in the spiritual world. Seeing clouds move under your feet is a dazzling feeling!

My lovely angel whom I have the purest love forever. When I first got to heaven my lil' sister had her angels, so I was hoping I would have angels, too.

When I first saw my angel, we had eye contact, I knew she was "special." I felt the purest love from her, without her saying a word to me. I looked over to my lil' sister and she said, "Man, Big Brother, she is beautiful! That's your type, too! And she's looking at you!" To think I could love someone that quickly and feel their love was astounding. When she flew down to meet me, her hair was blowing when there was no wind. It was mind-blowing. Then, with the softest tone, she said, "Hello, Quest. I'm S'rlove (Sure Love). I'm your angel here in heaven. I'll be with you all day and when you return one day." Take who you love and times that by a million. I was in awe! Around her I felt so loved.

What is the mirror of life?

If you stood in front of a fifty-foot-long by twelve-foot-high flat screen, that's how the mirror of life looks. Very flat!

While being floatless, I tried to touch it, but it moved back. When my lil' sister stood in front of it, it moved forward to touch her. I recall saying, "It's a TV, Keisha! What else could it be?"

I didn't have a clue. It was a "mirror." When she touched it and it came on, I was speechless. I couldn't move! When it started flashing, at first I couldn't see anything except white flashes. When I started believing it was a mirror, the flashing started to slow down into pictures of when my lil' sister was a child all the way up to her passing. It was like standing in front of a movie screen. We enjoyed it, laughing and smiling, the whole time, while watching my lil' sister's life flash before us.

How do I feel?

There are no words to describe how I feel, but I feel so special, that God let me experience heaven with my lil' sister. Today I have so much love for everyone. My heart goes out for those who are in need. I wish I could help everyone. I can love everyone freely. My spirit is at a high level at times. I believe in myself highly at everything I try to do, never once telling myself I can't do something. You too have to believe in yourself before anyone else believes in you. Have faith. I always do. I'm not perfect, but I strive higher, just to be close to it.

How did you get your psychic abilities?

First of all, I couldn't fathom the spiritual transmissions when I was younger. It took the death of my lil' sister to open my spiritual eyes and see things I couldn't fathom. I could dream about heaven, but what would I really see? Our minds can't fathom what heaven looks like. I am so blessed to have taken this journey to paradise, the angels, heaven clouds and most of all heaven!

My psychic abilities were instilled in me as a baby. Through the years they have developed into something special. My "Holy Mission" to heaven and to return here on earth with "psychic transmission" has altered my life immensely. My love for people has increased. I wanted to know more about my surroundings. I'm fascinated! I've always been in denial about seeing and listening to angels Sometimes I wear sunglasses, just so I can see the vivid stars that form into human shapes.

I've been given the ability to know many things that the average person cannot understand. I just want to show my kindness and appreciation, and use my psychic gifts to enlighten the world with divine light.

Trying to Move On

On February 26, 2009. a day after my lil' sister was buried, trying to move on was very difficult for us and for those who lost a loved one. We had to go over to her house and remove everything she touched. The way I think now, my spiritual connections could touch something that she touched and could see her using it. So, going to her house would be special to me and painful at the same time.

Luckily, my dad got there first with my brother, O'Shea. My lil' sister's daughter's father and Daryl were there as well. There wasn't much stuff that had to be moved. My dad was having a hard time with the move. My mother took most of my lil' sister's belongings. Her heart told her to give them away to people in need. My mother was trying to move on, but this was her baby.

My sister Ty was having a hard time as well. My lil' sister and she worked together, riding to work every day was their normal routine. Now her ride to work would be different. My lil' sister used to send her e-mails once a day. Now she is left with old e-mails. How do you move on? How do I move on?

As I sat in my truck, driving back to my house, I have so much on my mind, I didn't know where to start. I started writing down everything I experienced on paper. I really didn't know how to move on. Some days I would cry so hard, I'd just go to sleep afterwards, hoping that when I got up this would all be a bad dream. I would call my lil' sister's phone just to hear her voice, hoping she'd pick up, sometimes calling back to back. I was really in denial that my lil' sister had died. Not my lil' sister! Not my Little Keisha! When you lose a friend, you still cry and you're saddened for their family, but just think what they're going through. The same thing I'm going through losing a loved one. It really hurts the heart. I never spoke to a therapist about my experience of losing my lil' sister. I have spoken to my parents or Ty. Their love helped me to focus so I could tell this heavenly event. We all have changed from my lil' sister's death. We're more spiritual now than ever before.

My lil' sister's death had broken our hearts. There was hope. All I could feel was hope in my heart from my experience. We started loving each other again, this time from the bottom of our hearts. Love was in the air and we all needed it. We all had to love again. We all got out of the house. We went to the restaurants all the time as a big family. It felt weird not having my lil' sister there. I knew she was going to walk through the door at any moment. "Hello, everybody," she'd say with a smile!

Not anymore. Now it's just great memories. I could hear her and if I closed my eyes, I could see her. Her love makes me feel better inside and out.

I could tell she wanted to cry, but she couldn't.

My lil' sister said, "At least I told everyone I loved them before I died." My lil' sister and I had spoken the week before she died every day. I would tell her "I love you" before she would finish a sentence.

My lil' sister said, "What's wrong with you, boy? Are you dying or something? You tell me, 'I love you' before we're finished talking." She even told Ty that she thought something was going to happen to me! In fact, it would be her, not me that death took away. She called me that Sunday night to tell me that my son, Devin, was there with her, watching the NBA All Stars Game, just letting me know he was there and safe.

She spent the next day with Ty, and the next day with Dad, dancing and laughing with him at his house. She called me Tuesday with this question, "Is Goofy a dog or a walrus? I'll bet you a dollar he's a walrus." She called me back in a minute, laughing, "I owe you a dollar, Big Brother!"

I told my friend I had a bad feeling about Keisha. Did I know she was going to die? I didn't want to think about it, but yes, I couldn't tell how I knew. The thought made me cry day and night. I asked my lil' sister, "How do you feel?"

"Good," she answered.

I asked her, "Are you depressed?"

"No," she responded

God was telling me something I couldn't make sense of. I shouldn't have gone to see her in person. That's in my mind every day, every night.

My lil' sister wrote a book *Who I Am*. It just came out months before her death. She had the same gift as me, but who could understand what she and I went through every day. She helped others get their lives in order. She had an out-of-body experience as well. Who could she tell this to? Who would listen to her? Would you think she was crazy? Yes! But, I didn't because I had them too. If you have an out-of-body experience, tell someone; you are not alone. You're not different. God has allowed you to have these experiences.

My lil' sister was alone, not telling us, but writing it in her book. What I know now won't bring her back, but I can now help someone who's going through what we've been through.

This is a wonderful book to help others see the good in their lives. My lil' sister is an angel and always will be. Her experiences were overwhelming, just like my experiences, but I'm sharing them with you. She didn't. She just kept to herself.

The week before she passed away, I could feel her energy just blasting at me. It overwhelmed me. I asked her several times if she was okay She replied, "Yes! What's wrong with you?" I just couldn't explain it to her then. I blamed myself every day afterwards for her death. That's why I took it so hard. When she came back to me the first thing she said was, "Big Brother, it's not your fault. Don't blame yourself." She knew.

I waited so long to get this book published. With what happened to me, I don't have to defend my experience. I've been touched by an angel; had an angel walk through me and most of all, God allowed me to experience heaven all day with my lil' sister.

I'm crying now as I tell you this because I'm so thankful/joyful that you get to share my extraordinary heavenly experience. I'm so honored to share this event. I've put my heart and soul into this book. Please feel my love and joyful tears on every page. I've cried on every page. I might cry when I meet you. I am here. I am alive, walking and talking because of God's heaven. It's so beautiful and peaceful. With every blink I take, I can visit heaven. God has blessed me with an extraordinary gift. You too will visit heaven someday. When that time comes, there's so many angels in heaven waiting for your call. They will come, they are real; their love is so pure. I've felt their love and I was touched by an angel.

I'll see you one day in heaven, and you, too, will see what I have already experienced.

Dad

When I was a kid, I thought my dad was the coolest man on earth. Blessed with good looks, green eyes, light skin, wavy hair, and personality and charm. My dad had me when he was seventeen. He was a basketball star in high school. His dream of becoming a professional basketball player was cut short due to my birth. He finished high school at Northwestern Senior High in Hyattsville, Maryland. He started working and still had love for the game. My dad didn't have a father growing up as a kid. In his days he had other men around him to guide him in the right direction. Being a dad was hard for him mentally. He didn't give up, but it made things harder for my mother. As I got older, I would look at my dad differently. As the years passed, learning from him at every moment, I had wanted to mimic everything positive about him. My dad could draw so well. He just never pursued it like he did basketball. My dad is very creative mentally. I can remember, at age five, he would have me stare at a spot on the wall for a few minutes. He said, "What did you see besides that spot?" I said, "A star." He burst into laughter. He said, "You're right! To someone else it's just a spot, but to you and I, it's a star!" That was the beginning of my creative eye and how I would look at things like trees, clouds and even water.

My dad and I would go outside and look at everything, trying to put a face on it. My mother disliked how he had me looking at things in the world differently. She said, "Stop doing that because people are going to think he's crazy!"

I was now a teenager with the gift of creativeness, thanks to my dad.

I remember my dad telling me that he had seen a ghost or a spirit when he was young. This spirit stood in the doorway as he played with his toys. What do you say when your dad tells you something like that?

First of all, your dad, you think, should have been scared of nothing at any time. So, I thought my dad was very spiritual, however he was in denial about it. I've told my dad I love him and thanked him for bringing me into this world because he is who he is, which made me a well-rounded person. I know I made him proud of me for writing this book. It's because of my dad that I am who I am. The secret is coming!

Mother

When I was a child, I thought my mother was the prettiest lady in the world. She always had a smile on her face. Always smelled lovely, all the time. My mother had this scent like a "rose from heaven." She must have used that scent to make my dad fall in love with her! The two of them fell for each other, having me nine months later. My mother said I was special. She was so excited when she'd tell me that all the time. My mother attended Blair Northwestern High School, having me when she was fifteen years old. It was so hard for her. During those times, while her friends were all partying, she was at home taking care of a child.

When I was three years old, I remembered this like it happened a minute ago. I walked out of the house. I grabbed my toy, a yellow, steel truck. I crossed the street, walked up a steep hill. I got on top of this toy truck and rode down the hill at top speed – probably at 10 miles per hour. No brakes! I laughed the whole ride down the hill!

My mother never understood why or how I never got hurt on injured when traffic came both ways because the street is in a T-pattern! I shocked my mom and dad several times with this one! I would climb out of the window to feed the squirrels on the ledge of the roof, sometimes standing on the gutters with my arms out like I'm flying! I used to enjoy that so much! I sometimes can still feel it.

My mother and I talk about those days and just laugh! I love seeing her laugh. I used to do things to make her laugh really hard! You know, the kind of laughter that makes you choke, puts tears in your eyes. My mother is a very smart lady and good with her hands. She always told me never say, "I can't." Always try. Don't give up. I learned how to tint windows from my mother. Even if it didn't come out smoothly, she didn't stop trying to teach me. She even learned how to caulk around the windows in our house. It looked like cake frosting, but guess what? She tried. My mother made me a perfectionist.

My grandmother, Lorraine Delaney, "Mama," who was a beautiful lady, would care for my sister and me when my parents would be in school or at work. There wasn't anything we couldn't have to eat. Nothing she couldn't make, either! I remember she would kiss me so many times. She sat me on her lap and said, "You are a special person. Always show love for others who are so in need. I love you so much."

It was kind of hard being the special one, especially when there are other kids living in the house. But I was her "Special One." I've done so many incredible things, I had to be lucky, the luckiest kid in the world, just as my uncle Darryl would always tell me, even to this day.

{I've never told anyone this, this is the first} As I stood in front of my grandmother, I recall her saying, "I can't breathe! I can't breathe!" I stood there with tears in my eyes, hoping this was a joke. It wasn't! Every one was panicking! I stopped crying, watching my "mother" (sometimes I would call her that) hold her chest in such pain. She looked at me. I will NEVER forget that look. With tears in her eyes, I could feel her love deep within. All I knew, all I felt was her love. No matter what I did, she would always say, "I love you. You are special. Don't let anyone tell you differently"

I saw this glow around my grandmother. The same glow that I saw around my friend that I'd been playing with, his mother, and my little sister. That explains why my sister and my family thought I was talking to myself all the time, but I wasn't. I could see them all the time. Every time I went outside to play. He was there with the angels.

Moments later my grandmother would be taken to the hospital. That was the last time I saw her rocking in this red chair. She passed away that evening.

Days passed by and I remember asking my Auntie Flo, "Where's Ma at?" She replied, "Ma is in heaven." I asked, "Where is that?" With tears in her eyes, she explained, "Look outside in the sky."

I looked with tears in my eyes. My tears were from confession, not knowing what heaven was. That heaven had my grandmother and everyone was crying. I cry as I write this because the love she had for me was pure. She saw something in me at an early age. I can't forget how she used to tell me I was special. I was young but I could feel her love. To feel love like that was astounding. I'm not saying my mother's love isn't pure. My grandmother would look me eye-to-eye. Love in her eyes, her heart, her touch, that I so truly miss. The glow my Ma had was so amazing, but no one said they saw it around her. So, how could I see it? Maybe that's why our love was a spiritual love. Her eyes were so wonderful. I could see myself in them. I always loved looking at her.

I love you so much Momma, and I wish you could see me now in my walking life. I can hear you in my spirit world. I feel your love deep within me.

Due to my grandmother's passing, my mother took on more responsibilities. We stayed there at the house for another two years.

My parents moved from Takoma Park to Hyattsville. I was now five or six years old. My mother and father spent long hours at work. My sister and I had clothes and toys, but were missing love — that grandmother love. My mother's sister, Auntie Flo came over to care for us while mom and dad worked. We had so much fun with Auntie. I grew closer to Auntie because she looked more like my grandmother than all of them. There was that love I so adored. Every time she would leave, I would cry so much. I'd cry myself to sleep. I had my sister there to comfort me at times. The thought of my grandmother leaving me was so heartbreaking to me. I never recovered from her death. To be attached to my auntie at times became hard for my mother to be second place. I started hanging with my mother more often. The love was growing deeper with her. I could feel my grandmother's love through my mother. I never told her this before.

My mother, sister and I would race from the car to the house.

My mother would always let us win! She had this laugh that would make you laugh. I love her laugh so much. I wish I could hear it all the time.

I told my sister that I would do anything for her. We shared so much together. We were raised like twins, always dressing alike. Always! As we got older, you couldn't break us apart. We were one! One heartbeat.

My dad would spend time with us when he wasn't working. My dad is the creative one. This is where I perfected his trait that he taught my sister and I. My dad would have us stare at an object such as clouds, trees — you name it. He used to say, "You have to be creative and have a creative eye and mind. If you develop this trait, you have to perfect it. Doing this will make you see things other people can't see."

My dad was creative with art, handwriting, and painting. He was in my life every hour, every day, doing something creative. If you don't know what that means, let me tell you. You have to look at something, for example, a cloud, and tell him what you see. He could see it. We couldn't until we focused. Once you focused, you could see everything and anything. My mother would tell him, "You'll make those kids seem crazy to others," she sometimes would shout! "Stop doing that!" So, he stopped. We would tell him what we saw at times and he would look without saying a word. He would nod his head up if we were right, or down if we were wrong. His creativeness made me strive harder to see what he saw quicker. With a blink of an eye I became better. I wanted to be perfect at doing this. I wanted to be "a perfectionist" at everything my dad would teach or show me, from creative art or images, to everything I do. I wanted to perfect it. With my skills so on point, I became better at what he showed me.

My Grandmother

My dad's mother, Catharine Clark, was a spiritual lady. I loved her dearly. I miss her today and always will. A grandmother's love is always different. She would give me things my mother wouldn't. It was all love. I remember her telling me I was special and I wasn't like other kids. I didn't know what she meant by that as a kid, but once I grew up and came into my teenage years, I knew what she was talking about. I would talk to her about my dreams and that I could fly in my dreams. I would help people in my dreams get out of trouble or danger. She really enjoyed me telling her about my dreams until one day I told her I dreamt of people who had died. These people were lost and needed help. I would listen to them talk and sometimes laugh. She never once said I was crazy or just making this up because it was too vivid in detail. I used to see this gold glow around people who were near death, but didn't know it. I tried blocking this out of my mind because it was too hard for me to fathom. As I got older, I blocked a lot of things out of my mind, but it came back again. This time I told my Granna. I recall her saying I was her special grandson and one day I would know why. That day would come too soon for me. As she lay in the hospital bed, very sick, she would ask me, "Do you see that glow around me?" I started crying, but she said it was okay "It will just be our secret," until now because she did have that glow around her.

When I heard my grandmother's voice, I would get chills, and then I felt this warm breeze. I've never told anyone until now. I heard my grandmother's voice one night in the summer time. My parents, Ty, and I were riding in my mother's Chevy Impala, '64. This car was heavy: the hood, trunk and the doors. We drove up to the "4400 Club," a local club in North Brentwood. My parents asked for two sodas and a bag of chips. Normally, this club was busy, cars going up and down! But it wasn't that busy when we pulled up to the drive-thru window. I noticed a flash of light by my door. I tried to put my window down, but it was broken. That flash of light was trying to tell me something. This flash of light looked like a human face. I was so fascinated by his face.

I opened the door, but my parents were pulling off. I didn't want to say anything, so I tried to hold onto the door. The flash followed us. We made a u-turn, then…out swung the door, and out swung me! Aaaaaaaaah! "Go get him, Louis!" Oh my God! Go get him!" My mother yelled this over and over again. My mother and sister started crying. "Hurry up and get him! Oh my God! Are you okay, sweetie? Talk to me!"

When we turned the corner my door swung open, causing me to fall out and tumble over and over. "I'm okay, Ma," I'm okay."

"No, you're not, baby! You can't be! You tumbled like fifty feet." I can still see the shock and confusion on my parents' faces. Still in shock, my mother rushed me in the house. "Okay, Baby, I know you're hurt," she said, holding her face with both hands, "Please tell me where you're hurt at. How come you're not bleeding? How come he's not bleeding, Louis? He should be bleeding! He doesn't have any scratches on him!"

This is impossible! I remember looking at my parents and my sister's faces. They were amazed! "You scared us so bad. Thank God there were no cars coming down the street, they would've drove right over top of you!" I tried to tell them what happened, but they kept talking over me.

My mother told her sister and the whole family knew. My dad told his mother and sister. The whole town knew what happened to me. What they didn't know is that an angel came from the side of the car where I was sitting; he looked me right in the face and covered me so I wouldn't get hurt. I saw this bright orange light. It happened so fast that my dad didn't notice I was pointing to the angel. Even when I was three years old, the angel that was out there on the ledge with me was the same angel who saved me from this accident that day. No one ever knew an angel saved my life until now. I can talk about this event now, but back then who could I have talked to? Who would have believed me? I mostly stayed to myself afterwards, which made me even shyer.

I remember sitting in the living room watching my neighbor play with a Frisbee, throwing it up in the air and catching it. Man! Wow! That looks like fun! I asked my Auntie Flo if I could go outside and play with him. She said I could, and I ran outside. "Hey what's your name," I asked.

"Brian," he said.

"Show me how you do that. That looks like so much fun!"

He called me by my name, "Quest, catch!"

"How do you know my name?" I asked.

"Oh, your sister told me."

"Well, let's finish playing, Brian," I said. He showed me so many tricks with this Frisbee. One day he threw it up in the air so high, it looked like a bird! Wow! What was amazing to me was that I never saw him catch it. It was in his hands before I blinked. He would do this trick every time I saw him. Brian was around eight or nine years old. I was like seven or eight. Brian would knock on the patio doors for me. Tap! Tap! Tap! He would usually come around the same time every day. Some days I couldn't go outside so I had to watch him from inside my house.

My dad watched him with me do all these Frisbee tricks and really was impressed. He would just walk away from the patio doors, shaking his head.

"Can I go outside, Daddy," I asked.

"Yeah, take your sister, too," he relented. I really didn't want my sister playing with us, but since she already told Brian my name, she must have played with his sister before. His sister was seven, but she and I never played together. We came outside and I ran down the grassy field so I could catch the Frisbee from Brian. He threw the Frisbee down the grassy field toward me, but this time the Frisbee drifted so slow I could see it spinning, then *whoosh!* The Frisbee went to normal speed! With my sister looking on, I had to catch it.

"Yes! That was awesome, Brian!" I yelled. "That was awesome! Did you see that?"

She looked at me but didn't say anything. She kept playing with her dolls. "How did you do that trick, Brian?" I threw the Frisbee back to Brian so he could do it again. *Whoosh!* The same slow trick. "How did you do that, Brian!" I yelled.

"Brian?" my sister asked.

"You didn't see that Frisbee trick?" I asked.

"What Frisbee trick? You don't even have a Frisbee!"

"Brian! Come here, show my sister the Frisbee trick," I demanded. "She don't believe you can do it again, Brian." I wanted him to come closer.

"Who's Brian?" she asked.

"Brian! You told Brian my name!" I yelled. "No, I didn't!"

"Sure you did. How would he know my name if you didn't tell him?" I turned around to call for Brian. Brian started walking toward us. "Watch, wait till he shows you this trick," I instructed her. As Brian got closer, something amazing started to happen. Every step Brian took playing with the Frisbee, he became transparent. I could look straight through him, causing me to wonder how he'd done that trick with my sister looking on. As he got closer to us, he vanished in midair. "Now, that's a magic trick!" I yelled.

"What magic trick?" she asked.

"You saw what he done!" I insisted.

"He who? Why are you talking to yourself? I'm telling Daddy because you're scaring me," she said.

"Wait! The kid that threw me the Frisbee, Brian! I've been playing with him for weeks," I demanded.

"No! You've been playing outside with yourself for weeks," she insisted.

"You saw me run down the grassy field to catch the Frisbee."

"What Frisbee? You ran down the grassy field and started yelling, 'That's an awesome trick!' But you didn't do no trick. I was looking at you swinging your arms up and down, like you was throwing something," She explained.

"Yeah, a Frisbee!"

"What Frisbee? You're scaring me! I'm going back in the house and telling Daddy!"

"Don't! I was joking with you! I wasn't talking or playing with no one. I'm sorry," I said. When she went back in the house, I turned around to see if I would see Brian. I did, but he was walking down the hill, still transparent. If my sister didn't see him, maybe I didn't see him, but I knew I caught that Frisbee! I stopped believing what I saw when my sister questioned me about Brian. My level of spiritual connection with Brian faded, causing him to become transparent. All I knew was that I'd been playing with Brian for weeks. I was very confused, upset and very nervous. I became very shy and would play by myself; not even playing with my sister. I was lost in my soul. I kept having dreams about Brian, my grandmother, and my first friend. I never knew his name. Maybe Brian was his name? Maybe that was when I was younger. They looked much alike. Was that Brian who saved me from falling out of the car? It looked like Brian. I couldn't tell anyone what happened to me because they would think I'm crazy. I kept this secret about Brian to myself until now.

I would keep everything I heard and saw, spiritually, to myself for years. I was in denial, and therefore my spirit connection was dead. I became even more shy. I wasn't talking that much to my family. I really just stayed to myself. I was always close with my sister, Ty, yet I just knew I couldn't tell her everything. I became afraid of the dark because I started hearing voices again. I used to put cotton in my ears so I couldn't hear spirits. I blocked everything out. My mother got this dog from the pound. I'm not sure if my mother could tell or feel my sadness. That dog made me open up. When we walked in the dog pound, it felt like I could feel these dogs' sad energy. Even with their tails wagging, I felt their abuse, their sadness. We came across this beautiful dog. He was a shepherd and husky mix. We picked him, and he came home with us. We named him "Max." We played with him every day. It was my and my sister's duty to care for him. Max really brought happiness in the family for my sister and me. I felt connected to him for some spiritual reason. I used to take him on long walks just talking to him. I really felt like he understood me. You know animals have those incredible senses. I felt like Max could protect me from anything.

Keisha was very smart to be four years old. Her level of thought was very impressive. Keisha and I came into the house to do our homework and clean the floors. I panicked because I couldn't find my keys. I recall looking everywhere in the house – upstairs, downstairs. My mother was coming home soon! Keisha touched me and said, "I'll find them for you. They're still in the door."

I countered, "No they're not!" We opened up the door slowly, and there they were!

"That wasn't it," she said. "Normally you open the door and take ten steps and put them on the table."

I asked, "Why do you count numbers?"

She said, "I always count numbers! They—"

"They who?" I asked.

"They tell me numbers all the time. Sometimes I see them." I was getting nervous and scared. When she told me this, it sent chills down my whole body. I didn't want her going through what I went through as a kid. I kind of knew what she was trying to say, because when I was fourteen, my deceased grandfather Leroy Delaney came to me in a dream. I convinced myself it was a dream. I was sleeping in my bed, and he walked into my room.

He said, "Hey, you want to go to the Hot Shoppes with me?" I replied, "Yeah, why not. You're my grandfather, but we should ask Ma first."

He said, "No, we don't wanna wake her up, she needs her rest. She has a hard day ahead of her." When we walked through the door, I turned into a kid again, a five-year-old kid with his grandfather. I could not stop laughing because I thought it was the coolest magic trick. He said, "Sssssshhh, not so loud. Watch this trick." We floated down the stairs and walked through a metal door. Wow! All I thought was how amazing it was.

"How did we do that Dadda?"

"Shhhhh, you'll wake your momma," he said.

We got into a 1974 station wagon, the one he always drove. We drove to the bottom of the hill and turned the corner. We then got into a white Chevy pick up truck with blue seats. We drove to the Hot Shoppes in Takoma Park. This was his favorite restaurant. He said I could get anything I wanted. I noticed a lady with angel eyes looking at me. I felt her touch my soul. She walked up to my grandfather and asked, "Mr. Delaney?"

"Yes, Sugar." She couldn't stop looking at me. As I looked around the room, everyone had this gold realm behind them. It looked like everyone was standing or sitting in front of the car's headlights. My experience with what I saw wasn't on point. Now I've seen this glow before with my grandmother and friends. I can recall everything I saw before, like each person's outfit; the manager with coffee stains on his blue tie; the run in one of the waitresses' stockings; the lady's hair net that wouldn't stay intact.; the older White man who was short on money (thirteen cents short). The waitress still gave him his coffee, free. I noticed my granddad, "Dadda" adjusting his pants with a white patch that read, "Delaney, Leroy" on it. His green pants, brown boots and white t-shirt, green shirt also had a patch with "Leroy" on it. He was wearing a hat and a brown belt. He had one grapefruit with a spoon and one coffee with four sweet-n-low. He asked for more sweet-n-low, with a laugh. He said, "I don't suppose you have that much sugar, but who knows, it's just you and me here, son." He paid for his meal with two dollars and fifty-five cents. I had ice cream, but what was amazing, we didn't eat anything with our mouths! No one did. But I could taste it!

As we returned to the station wagon, I could hear my mother's voice calling me. My granddad asked me not to tell anyone what had happened until the time was right. My mother's voice got louder. I looked at my granddad, and he disappeared right in front of me. I could hear him, "You love your mother and father always, okay? Love you, son." My granddad never told my mother he loved her when she was growing up. I wanted to tell my mother so much that "dada" said he "loves you and thanks for caring after him when your mother passed away." I kept that secret. I kept that secret for so long.

I did tell her I had a dream about her father. I told her I woke up so confused because everything that happened felt so real to be a dream. The colors, everyone happy, joyful and the glow.

She replied, "That was a dream." I knew I had heard my grand-dad's voice, but now was not the time to tell her. She wouldn't understand. She wasn't impressed with my dreams. I felt at that moment the hurt from her spirit of talking about her father that made her feel lonely. I could see my mother's eye tearing up. After seeing her eyes tear up, I didn't want to say any more. I didn't want to see my mother hurt. She was crying inside with no help. How was I able to feel her feelings. I didn't know at the time. I couldn't feel anything when my dad came around. He was blocking my mother's energy.

My grandfather came to me so many times afterwards that I though I was dreaming. The message I got from his visits was "love!" He showed me that he could love people and he wasn't an angry old man, like people thought he was. He loved all of his kids. He never told them he loved them, but he told me. The events I had with him were wonderful. He kept a picture of his children in his wallet. He would show this photo to everyone who would look, even at the Hot Shoppes.

When my granddad passed away, my mother started spending a lot of time by herself, but my lil' sister gave my mother the strength to continue to find happiness with my sister by her side all the time. They became one; did everything together. My lil' sister was around seven. Ty and I were seventeen. By that time I was very much into myself spiritually. I vowed not to tell anyone what I thought; how I controlled my thoughts. I could feel people's sad energy. I found myself helping people who needed my help and helping my class-mates who didn't believe in themselves. I saw the inner beauty of their spirit. I noticed as I looked in people's eyes, I could feel their pain. "Eyes to the soul." I used to avoid eye contact all the time. Who could I tell what I was experiencing? I didn't want to believe my lil' sister had this glow, but she did. But there was one strange thing—she was alive! My granddad had the glow as well. Here my little sister was alive and had the glow. I asked Ty, "When you look at Keisha, what do you see? Do you see a glow around her?"

She replied, "I don't see anything." I knew that it was only me.

Believe

It is I that must
Believe I have
Great talents
That I can achieve.
If I fail myself
I will not succeed.
I must believe
Deep within so I
Can achieve what's
Within.
It is I that must…
Believe

Seventeen

When I was seventeen I was going through so much in my life that my spirit level had risen to a point that everyone I passed in the school hallway had problems. Some people I knew lost their parents, aunts, uncles, friends, and teachers. I felt like my head was going to explode. There were so many lost souls who were in need of help. Some days when it was very stressful on me, I would go over my girlfriend's house. She and her grandmother were spiritual.

One afternoon we sat on the sofa in the living room. Out of the corner of my eye I saw a smoky shadow. I was in denial about the shadow, but she asked me, "Did you see that?"

I said, "Yeah!" We both became afraid and left the apartment. She said her grandmother and her saw all the time, but just blocked it out. I wanted to know more but she refused to talk about it. I didn't know how to express myself back then because I was so shy. There were shadows that moved all around me that I could see. My girlfriend saw them too. That's why I loved her so much then. Sometimes she acted like she didn't see them. I believed she was in denial too because again, who's gonna believe us and who could we tell this to? My smell became much more sensitive. I could smell my grandfather's aftershave all the time. I felt like he was watching my mother even when I went over my auntie's house. It didn't matter which aunt or uncle's house, I could smell my granddad. I could hear his laughter too. All of these events were driving me crazy. To block out spirits were hard for me. I felt alone! Not loved! I felt scared all the time, knowing I couldn't tell my parents or Ty.

But my lil' sister knew! She knew what I was going through because she too could see spirits and angels. I could feel what my lil' sister was feeling. She made me believe that what I saw and heard was normal because she thought it was normal. But she's only seven years old, what did she know about spirits? I asked myself over and over, why me? I never got a chance to ask my lil' sister what she saw and heard as a child. I overheard her talking to her friend about what she would see and hear. She was in the room playing with her tea set. She said, "Why do you always come play with me when no one's around?" Now, I'm standing in the kitchen behind the refrigerator. "You have to meet my Big Brother, he's funny. You'll love him. All the girls think he's cute, but he's not cute, cuz he's my Big Brother."

At first it scared me because I went through the same experience with "Brian." I poked around the refrigerator, "Don't go!" she told her friend. I asked who she was talking to. She gave me this look, like I knew already. She sat there and started to cry. I asked why she was crying. She said, "Because you scared my friend away." I didn't have to ask any more questions! I knew my lil' sister could see spirits because I had the same look on my face. My lil' sister became more aware of her surroundings. I was very impressed. We started what my dad called, "Creative Eye." Just looking at everything: carpets, towels, rocks, paper bags, trees, clouds, water, and so on. We would look at things and see who would come up with a picture first.

Things became fascinating to us. We could see so much more than the eye could see. We were so amazed by our abilities. We would ask others what they saw. It was nothing like how we saw it. My sister Ty had that gift for the creative eye too. My lil' sister could see thing so much faster. That, to me, was amazing since she was only seven years old.

My dad would be home most of the time, but he and I weren't on that "father-to-son" level. I really didn't think he loved me. I couldn't really talk to him about any thing except basketball or boxing, and still, he was in his own world. Now, if we talked about using your creative eye, he seemed to be more into it with me. I felt pushed away. Something happened to my dad that probably scared him and he didn't know how to handle it. You see, my dad saw spirits when he was a child, too. He never said anything to us until my lil' sister died. He tried to tell us this when my sister and I were younger, but we just thought he was smoking something. He was in denial too for thirty-five years. We didn't see eye-to-eye anymore. I loved my dad dearly, but he knew the things he chose to do in his life affected the whole family. For that reason, I didn't want to be a part of it. My mother and father never cursed at all. I'm so thankful I never heard curse words from their mouths. I could feel the negative vibes from both my parents. My father had my mother in a "Panic attack" state for all the issues they were going through. As a teenager I didn't know what to think of the whole "speechless experience." Speechless! They were! This really affected my sister and me. My lil' sister was too young to understand what was going on.

We all were at odds with each other. This was the time I needed my parents and sister the most. The speechless event affected Ty very hard just as it did me. She became shy and distant from my parents and me. I felt so lost from not talking to her. We used to talk about everything every day. I felt like everyone was avoiding me. How do you avoid your son, your brother? I didn't feel loved or wanted in the house. I recall going to bed and just crying myself to sleep. I could hear my dad's voice within saying, "Stop crying, boy! Don't cry." But I was and have been very sensitive, so I cry easily when events like this get to me. I lay there, crying. I got up and walked downstairs. I opened the door and there was my dog, looking at me. I felt comfort lying there with Max, even though he couldn't talk. I really felt we were communicating back and forth. I cried myself to sleep just holding him all night. So, every time I wanted to cry, I would go sleep with him to comfort and show me love. He showed me love every day. I really had a special bond with my Max. I was thinking, *If anything would happen to Max, I wouldn't know what to do.*

My First Out-Of-Body Experience

Growing up in the household became very stressful. I felt unloved and unwanted. My mother and I were continually arguing with each other. She would blame me for not living up to her standards, which made me a perfectionist. The tension between my mother and me intensified, and I made up my mind that I couldn't live there anymore.

The house became so sad for me. I wanted to take my own life. I really felt I was so alone and unloved. It came to a point that I didn't want to look anything like my dad. He never told me he loved me. My mother never told us she loved us because she was never told that by her parents. Love is all I wanted, and I wasn't getting it. Seeing things and hearing things was too much for me. I didn't know how to handle it. I took ten pills that night, planning to die. I dreamed that night that I was walking my dog and he spoke to me. He said, "If you die, who's going to walk and feed me? I love you. You love me. You gotta get up now." I got up, thinking I was dead already. As I was lying there I could see myself hovering over my body. Seeing this for the first time scared me. I didn't know that was me because I looked different. As I watched myself crying, I walked through my door and my sister's door. I could see her lying there peacefully and so happy. I went downstairs and saw my parents. They also were sleeping peacefully. I thought about my lil' sister and how I couldn't leave her, that she loved me so much. I retuned back to my room, watching myself crying and shivering.

To travel around the house so freely was amazing. To walk through doors and walls was unbelievable. Seeing myself cry was like standing in front of the mirror and waving to myself and you feel myself waving back, but my mirror image was not waving back.

I started shaking; then I stopped. I also noticed that I wasn't moving. Did I die? That's all I was asking myself, "Did I die? Did I die? I don't want to die, God. I'm too young. I just want someone to love me." I wasn't moving at all. She came into the room. She started shaking me over and over. When I saw her, my first thought was, why is she in my room crying over that body lying there on the bed? I hovered over the lifeless body and then I noticed it was me! That's why I didn't notice myself because I was all delirious. I believed I was lying there motionless. I saw myself crying and taking my last breath. I watched myself lying there. I regretted not telling my lil' sister that I loved her. At that moment I could hear my lil' sister's voice. I fell right on myself, causing me to gasp for air and I started choking. I awoke not feeling the same, but really happy. She was very happy that I woke up. I could feel this experience scared her so much. All I could do was hug her. I really didn't know what had happened. At least I told myself that! I told myself all the years that it was a dream—nothing more than a dream!

I woke up saying that over and over to my sister so she would think I had a bad dream. I was confused and lost at that moment. This was my first out-of-body experience. When it happened, I was in denial. I would find myself in the same loveless moments again with my parents. I felt like I didn't have anyone. My girlfriend and I split up for good. Ty was still going through depression. I really believed I was too. I just didn't know how to control it. My parents were on some other level at this point in time. Their love went two different ways. I hated it! I started thinking about death again. Would I be missed more in death than alive?

No Love

I had an after school job working at Wendy's from 3:00 to 10:00 p.m. I wanted to work all night because I didn't want to go home. I began to have those thoughts again: If I die, would people cry? Would they love me more when I'm gone? I'd seen entertainers die, and fans would love them more. I would walk home thinking, "I'm going to jump off this bridge. I had already envisioned what was going to happen. I would jump off this bridge, get hit by the biggest truck, and wouldn't feel any pain. All the news media would cover the accident because I was a teenager. My parents would love me more now that I was gone. I would be talked about every day. They would only think about the good times we had when I was a child. Everyone would be crying over my death, but they should have told me they loved me! That's all I wanted to hear, "I love you!" Why wait until I'm gone to say I love you, like so many people do?

Each step seemed so slow. Why is every car and truck going so slow? Even the wind in the air stopped. The stars became brighter— a brilliant shine. The moon became touchable. It was so close that I could see dips and craters. I walked toward the bridge and grabbed the rails. I couldn't explain what was happening at the moment because I was in denial of the spirit world. I stood up on the bridge and told myself I was going to jump. I jumped! All I saw was white!

I felt a tug on my arm. Wow! That didn't hurt! Finally! No more school! No more problems! Just like that! I thought about my mother. How could I do that to her and my sisters? Are they going to hate me because I'm gone? I wanted to cry, but I couldn't because I just killed myself! What was I thinking??? all I wanted was love, that's all, and for someone to love me. I could hear my lil' sister, "Why did he kill himself? That's my big brother in that coffin in the white suit and yellow tie. Why is he holding his sunglasses? Why are there so many people here to see him in his coffin? Why is dad crying so much? Why did big sister faint? Why would you do this, Big Brother? Why? I love you! I love you!" Crying over my motionless body.

The truck crushed every bone in my body, but I looked good in my white suit and a touch of yellow. There were so many people there all coming out to see me. I didn't understand how so many people were showing their love for me but didn't do it while I was alive. Again, I heard my lil' sister's voice, "Why Big Brother? Why? Why?" I started to hear a man's voice. "Why? You don't have to do this, Quest." I remember thinking, *If I died, then why am I not in heaven yet? Why do I still see a white light?*

"Quest, come down. You don't have to do this!" Again, I heard my lil' sister's voice, "I love you, Big Brother!" *Whoosh!* As I stood there on the ledge of the bridge, I started crying to myself. The male voice I heard was a driver who had stopped and shined his high beams on me. He was talking to me the whole time.

I said, "I thought I jumped. How did I get back up here?"

"You didn't jump, Quest," he told me.

"I did because I felt a tug and saw all this white."

"No, Quest! I grabbed you. You saw your future before your eyes when you blinked from the lights. What is your mother going to say when she finds out you killed yourself? How about your dad?"

"My dad doesn't love me! They don't love me! No one loves me! I don't wanna live because I'm not loved. I hurt so much inside because I want someone to love me. That's all," I responded.

"I love you, Quest. Your sisters love you; your parents love you." He grabbed my arm and asked me to step down from the bridge.

"How do you know my name?" I asked. He put his hands on my shoulders. I could feel the warmth from his hands.

"You are loved, Quest! From this day on you will be loved by all who come in contact with you." When he said that, I stopped crying immediately. I turned around to see him face-to-face, but the headlights were so bright. I only saw his silhouette.

"Thank you for saving me because I almost jumped." Looking over the bridge, watching the biggest truck pass underneath, I exclaimed, "Wow! That would have hurt!"

"You are loved, Quest," he reassured me.

Looking back at him, I asked, "How do you know my name?" Again, all I could see were the bright lights as I tried to get a look at him. "Hello, how do you know my name?"

He wasn't there! He'd vanished with the headlights. I looked up and down the street. There wasn't even a car for miles around. I didn't know it then, but that was my first Angel experience. He was an angel. He knew everything about me and my family. I could feel the warmth from his hands when he touched me. I was kind of scaring myself, so I started walking home faster, thinking about what had just happened to me. It was not a dream. You can't dream walking across the street. Why could I hear my lil' sister's voice? I ran home so fast it was unbelievable. I came into the house and went right to the bathroom. My heart was beating so fast. I threw water on my face. WOW! As I looked in the mirror, I noticed my pupils were enlarged. I tried to relax, closing my eyes and counting. When I opened my eyes again, my pupils were still enlarged. I opened the door, and my lil' sister was standing there.

"What are you still doing up, Keisha?" I asked. She looked like she had been crying. I gave her a hug.

"Big Brother, I had a bad dream about you. You're the best Big Brother in the world, and I don't want nothin' to happen to you." Now could she have known what I just went through? The next morning, I wanted to tell everyone what had happened to me. I just didn't want to seem like a crazy person, so I didn't tell them about the event, not until now.

In December 1968, one Friday night, the sky was so clear you could touch every star in the sky. The moon was full and looking down on my parents. As they looked up in the sky they always noticed this one star. This wasn't just any star. This was a star of love that that seemed to follow them everywhere. This star of love made them love each other more. They used to look at the stars all the time, naming the ones that they knew of. One of the brightest stars seemed to communicate with them. They felt love come over their souls. My parents never told me this story. I always felt that I knew about the star in the sky—the star of love. My parents never thought that star would affect their lives forever.

Later on my parents went looking back up in the sky for that one bright star. However, it wasn't there, as if it had vanished. Looking at each other in disbelief, my parents were amazed and puzzled. My mother felt differently. She had this feeling come over her that she couldn't put into words. My father didn't know what to say as well. As they hugged each other and looked up in the sky, the star of love appeared brighter than ever. That same feeling came back over my mother, but this time she touched her stomach. At that moment, I became a gift to my parents and the universe. I'm incarnated from a touch of God's heavenly light. I'm a special emissary with messages beyond all our knowing. I chose my parents for a reason – to gain their experiences and change the way they love one another; show them my way of loving someone deep within and push away their negativity. My instincts and intuitive senses have been with me since I was born. I display an unusual set of psychological attributes that parents, teachers and doctors can't explain. I am unique.

Growing up, I was misunderstood all the time by my parents and others. I had special events in my life that couldn't be explained. I didn't speak much because my thoughts would come at me so fast. I communicated telepathically. I was a phenomenal child with multiple talents. Only my parents have to believe what they saw with their own eyes. Don't treat me differently. Don't worry about what people and family say about me. Don't be in denial of what you see me do. Don't try and manipulate me or lie to me because I know when you do. I notice any hidden agendas from all. I see people and things others can't see. Love is very important to me, so always tell me you love me, no matter what. My intelligence and wisdom is far greater than others. Please understand that. I was born a philosopher. If you continue to let your negative energy smother my energy, you won't be aware of my gift. In the future I will return back to heaven only to come back again, only as a totally different being. My mission here on earth to help people who have a hard time after their loved one has crossed over. I've been sent to earth to teach my parents and others about spiritual truths. I'll be able to read your emotions, even if you try to hide them. I'll be very sensitive and detached from most people. Just honor the angel within me. Only love matters in the world.

My Spiritual Dream

On February 17, 2009, at 2:18 a.m., I woke up gasping for air. I started choking uncontrollably. I sat up on my bed and looked at my alarm clock.

"2:18 * 2:23 * 2:25*" I stood up and got a sip of water. I felt an emptiness in my heart for some reason. I put my hand over my heart and felt my heartbeat. It felt like I had two heartbeats; then it changed to one. I really felt different. I felt so alone! This feeling I was having, I couldn't explain. Maybe it was my dream? But this dream felt too real because I could feel it run through my soul. I felt like crying, but I didn't know why. I've been having the same dream for two weeks now. Maybe because I've been talking to my lil sister, Keisha, every day. But this night my dream was different. Every night I dreamt my lil' sister would be smiling, running toward me with her arms straight out, calling "Hey, Big Brother!" I would grab her and throw her up in the air. But not this night, she would be smiling, running toward me with her arms straight out, calling "Hey, Big Brother," but this time she ran through me, never once looking back at me, as if she didn't need me anymore.

After that dream, my mind and soul were lost. My thoughts were spinning around in my head so fast, like when you're a kid and an adult picks you up and spins you around in the air and places you on your bed. As I sat on the edge of my bed, visions of my little sister running through me over and over and over again. I tried running after her, and grabbing her, but I couldn't. She was happy, smiling and laughing, a flower in her hair and skipping off with this beautiful butterfly. As I stood there looking at her, I shouted her name, "Keisha! Come back! Where are you going? You can't leave me, Keisha!" She skipped off but it wasn't a normal skip, it was a happy skip, more like getting candy from the Dollar Store! The butterfly made her more at peace. The butterfly first touched her hand as if it was me. Then it settled on her shoulder. It then flew around her as they went into the light. I felt joy and peace.

As I woke up I was saddened because my lil sis ran through me. I couldn't move for a few minutes just stunned and shocked. I couldn't even swallow normally. My heart was beating faster and faster. I kept asking myself well, part of me was telling me that I was dreaming. So it was nothing but a dream. My heart felt alone at that moment (2:18 a.m.). I sat at the edge of my bed for several minutes. I should have called her, but I didn't. I really should have called. Not making "that phone call" affects me to this day. You're asking yourself, "Why would it affect him?" Because had I called my lil sis, she would have picked up the phone minutes before she died. That wasn't just a dream I had, it was real! It was her letting me know that she was okay and she didn't need Big Brotha to hold her hand anymore.

I didn't want to believe this or my dream, but it was true. Her spirit communicated with my spirit. I felt like I was the last person on earth. So many moments in my dream stained my brain. When I yelled for her, she kept skipping. She never looked back at me. This dream by far is the worst dream of my life. I've been dreaming since I was born, and this was the worst. No one or anything has ever passed through me, especially a loved one. If this ever happens to you, get up and call that person. Every day and every night I think about that "phone call." My lil' sis tells me spiritually, "It's not your fault, Big Brotha. God wanted me to come home. Don't sit here and cry over me. I'm okay, Big Brotha. I'm okay now." I sat there, scared and in disbelief. Scared because if she didn't pick up, then what if this was my gift of "the knowing?" Knowing when a person may pass over? I really didn't know what to think. No one knows when my lil' sis took her last breath, not even the doctors. But I know what time it was when everything happened that she couldn't control. What I also noticed from that dream was the surroundings. My lil' sis was skipping on the grass, which turned this real bright green. Out of nowhere roses bloomed everywhere as her skip slowed down.

Each rose sparkled with love. God was showing me how heaven looked, giving me a glimpse of it. I didn't understand it then like I do now. Looking back on it now, I fully understand what I was seeing. My thoughts of heaven changed for good. While staring at something in a daze, every blink was a glimpse of heaven My day in heaven with my lil' sis will remain with me for the rest of my lifetime. When my mind is clear and I'm relaxed and free, I will take several deep breaths, close my eyes, and I can see heaven. I do this several times a day. I love it! I love and thank God so much for my experience. Being in heaven makes me so at peace, joyful and more loving. I really hope you believe this book was meant for you to read and share my heavenly experience with family, friends and others around the world.

Keisha would be the first one to call me and tell me happy birthday. The night of my birthday I started to cry knowing I wouldn't hear my lil' sister's voice again. As my tears rolled down my face, I thought back over the last twenty-nine years and how my lil' sis has wished me a "Happy Birthday every year." As I walked from my bedroom to the dining room with tears streaming down, I felt a "breeze" right next to me touching my hands and face. I looked in the mirror and couldn't believe what I saw. No tears on my face! That breeze wasn't just a "gentle breeze," but my lil' sis was wiping away my sadness and tears.

"Happy birthday, Big Brother! I love you!" she whispers softly in my ear. "You thought you weren't ever going to hear my voice again, Big Brother? How can I forget what day this is?" I was totally in shock, hearing her voice again, knowing she was there with me.
My life's purpose is to spread "love" around the world. I want people to feel what I felt and envision what I've seen; have a clear understanding that if you show love, you will receive love. Everything in heaven that I've seen was a blessing from God.